Gottfried Richter

ART
and
HUMAN
CONSCIOUSNESS

Gottfried Richter

ART
and
HUMAN
CONSCIOUSNESS

Translated by Burley Channer and
Margaret Frohlich

Anthroposophic Press · Spring Valley, New York

Floris Books · Edinburgh

This book is a translation of the seventh edition of *Ideen zur Kunstgeschichte* published in 1982 by Verlag Urachhaus in Stuttgart, West Germany.

© 1982 Verlag Urachhaus Johannes M Mayer GmbH & Co KG Stuttgart

Copyright © Anthroposophic Press, Inc. 1985.

Published in North America by Anthroposophic Press, Inc., 258 Hungry Hollow Road, Spring Valley, N.Y. 10977

Published in the United Kingdom by Floris Books, 21 Napier Road, Edinburgh EH10 5AZ

Unites States Library of Congress Cataloging in Publication Data

Richter, Gottfried, 1901-
    Art and human consciousness.

    Translation of: Ideen zur Kunstgeschichte.
    Includes index.
    1. Art—History.   I. Title.
N5300.R54313 1985   709   84-28269
ISBN 0-88010-108-3

British Library Cataloguing in Publication Data

Richter, Gottfried
Art and human consciousness.
1. Art—History
I. Title   II. Ideen zur Kunstgeschichte. *English*
709   NS300

ISBN 0-86315-025-X

Printed in Great Britain
by Billing & Sons Ltd, Worcester

CONTENTS

PREFACE

Only a few years ago Suzi Gablik, in a book entitled *Progress in Art*, tried to establish a revolutionary new idea, observing that the changes occurring between pre-Renaissance, Renaissance, and Modern art are related to progressions in human consciousness perceptible today in the changing psychological structures of the growing child. The basis for her statements was the work of one of the leading child psychologists of our time, Jean Piaget. The idea that man's psychological progress through the ages is paralleled with some modifications in the progress of the growing human being today follows simply and logically upon observations made by embryologists, who long ago found in the metamorphoses of the fetus reflections of man's physical development in past ages. It is little known, however, that many decades ago Rudolf Steiner applied this law of biogenetics to the explanation of the mental and psychological development of the human being and that this insight was one of the many innovative ideas underlying the educational methods of the Waldorf schools, an international educational system founded by Rudolf Steiner in 1919. History and history of art as the history of human consciousness, and at the same time as a reflection of the student's own state of mind, has become the basis for all historical and art historical instruction in those schools. In addition, Steiner's thoughts on the history of human consciousness have inspired many writers in this field to give new dimensions to their presentations of past cultures. Of works written in the English language, one has only to think of the extraordinary studies of the history of language and thought written by Owen Barfield, especially his *Saving the Appearances* and *History in English Words*.

While many publications by writers steeped in Steiner's ideas deal with individual masters, cultures, or works of art, Gottfried Richter's *Art and Human Consciousness (Ideen zur Kunstgeschichte)*, here translated for the first time into English, has remained the only book in which these ideas are applied to a large survey of the history of art with systematic thoroughness. The fact that since its first appearance in 1937 it has undergone seven printings, and also a paperback edition by a major publisher, makes clear that this work has met a great demand, and yet it has remained virtually unknown outside those circles for which it was originally written, the teachers and pupils of the Waldorf schools and the members of the Christian Community, a religious movement also brought into being with Rudolf Steiner's assistance, in which Richter was a priest. The highly poetic language and the depth of Christian feelings expressed in this book may in fact create barriers for some, keeping them from recognizing the profound new insights into the history of art gained by Richter, who was trained as an art historian before he became a priest. The book is indeed an extraordinary proof of the fruitfulness of Steiner's new approach to history. It shows that one can achieve a new understanding of past ages not only through extensive learning—clearly evident in Richter's book—but through a penetrating analysis of major phenomena of a culture, reaching down to the deep structure or core of man's relationship to the world and to the spiritual cosmos around him. Richter uses primarily his profound understanding of architecture for this purpose but analyzes sculpture and painting as well, with much profit for the reader.

Steiner's approach and therefore also Richter's was nourished by the scientific and scholarly methods developed by Johann Wolfgang Goethe. For this great German poet and scientist of the eighteenth century, all investigations began with a patient and reverent contemplation and observation of the phenomena themselves, which then revealed to him what he called the *Urphänomene*, the archetypal phenomena, i.e., the mobile and flexible forces underlying a wealth of otherwise unrelated physical or psychological data. Consciously or unconsciously, Goethe's ideas have influenced European thought profoundly. One of the most influential schools of art history in our time, the Vienna school founded by Alois Riegl, is very close to Goethe's approach in its object-oriented and objective methods. Riegl's term *Kunstwollen* can be explained as the unconscious or half-conscious urge or striving perceived as the principal moving factor behind the appearance and character of a specific work of art, artist, artistic region, or period, thus representing an archetype. Hans Sedlmayr's expression "the critical phenomenon," meaning a phenomenon which by its extreme quality allows one to understand the structure of a larger whole, relates closely to Goethe's use of deformations or unusual developments in the plant or animal kingdoms to understand the

regular processes underlying larger groups of phenomena, again archetypal structures.

At the basis of these approaches to the understanding of art and of the
world is the experience that the human being can school his powers of
observation to such a degree that he can penetrate empathetically to the
seemingly invisible and often not quite explicitly or consciously expressed
aims and aspirations of a culture, of a person, or even of the life and
things of the world, and in doing this reach an objective reality. It is a
trust in man's power of the imagination and in his capacity for synthesis,
allowing the researcher to grasp the unifying forces behind the wealth of
outer phenomena. Art history dealing with "styles" of periods, nations,
and individuals has always expressed a belief in such unifying forces. In
art they become truly visible.

That art makes visible otherwise hidden cultural and psychological
forces has long been recognized and has made it a tool for the cultural
historian as well as the psychiatrist. It can be used for the diagnosis of an
age, a culture, or a patient. Yet diagnosis has to be trained! And this
training cannot rely on the mind or the eye alone but has to comprise the
whole human being. Thinking, feeling, and even the will have to be involved in the perception of the work of art. This is most evident in the
experience of architecture, where an ever-so astute analysis of the
groundplan cannot replace the feeling one receives from the light and
shade pervading the spaces and the actual muscular communion with the
whole that is experienced through walking around and into the building.
Yet sculpture and painting have to be perceived in the same way, down
into the bones! Art history, then, requires a constant training of all our
senses. The whole human being has to be transformed into a sense organ
whose findings can finally be expressed in conscious ideas and images.
Gottfried Richter is a master of this wholistic seeing. With agility he can
slip from observations of the eye to feelings and moral concepts. Scholar-
ship, art, and religion interweave into a poetic and coherent whole. And
yet this is not merely superficial brilliance. Every one of his ideas has
been gained by much looking, feeling, and thinking in front of or within
the very works of art or buildings he describes. The book is the result of
many long and loving meditations and distillations, so that at the end the
whole seems natural, simple, and clear and at the same time astonishing-
ly new and original.

Who would think, for example, of explaining the new feeling of Renaissance man by analyzing fifteenth century churches in Germany, which were still built in a typical Gothic language. And yet Richter can show us how within this tradition the artists create a new sense for space, and thus for the world, which is as characteristic of modern man as anything Italy had to offer at the same time. Richter's examples often come from the German world that surrounded him and with which he was deeply familiar, but his approach allows him to begin from any example at his disposal and to lead us from there as surely, and probably more profoundly, into the depth of the character of an age and culture as other art historians relying only on the well-known masterpieces traditionally considered the prime examples of their time.

Insights gained by the imagination with the help of all the faculties of the human being can often not be expressed with a rational language. Richter has to use analogies, parables, and pictures, following once again the example of Goethe, who in his attempts to grasp the ever-changing and transforming qualities of life had to rely on poetic imagery and did so not only with extraordinary virtuosity but also with a relentless sense for appropriateness and truth. "Alles Vergängliche ist nur ein Gleichnis" ("Everything transitory is but a likeness") ends the second part of his *Faust*, showing that the old Goethe experienced all the phenomena of the visible world as pure images for higher realities; images, moreover, in constant transformation. Goethe's doctrine of metamorphosis is, in fact, another part of Richter's method. As he guides us through the ages we can begin virtually to see how the Egyptian temple transforms into the Greek one and then into the early Christian basilica and finally into the cathedrals of the North, a series of continuous but at times radical transformations that are as logical and yet as astonishing as the developmental stages of the animal world or of the human embryo.

From a purely intellectual discipline Richter transforms art history into one that can stand at the center of a man's self-understanding. He weaves threads from art to psychology, philosophy, theology, economics, and even medicine or law. Of all these, the link to theology is the strongest. Richter was a priest and a Christian of unusually profound convictions. He deeply experienced the incarnation, death, and resurrection of Christ as central events in the history of the world. Christ was for him the highest divinity, the sun spirit who became man and united Himself with the earth, so that He can now begin to speak and act within and from the earth and within and through every human being willing to unite himself with Him. Richter shows how every artistic phenomenon can be seen in the light of this major event of human evolution. His findings correspond with those of Hegel, who by his classification of art into three forms corresponding to three great epochs—the symbolic, the classic, and the romantic—described in a completely different way and from a completely different point of view the same archetypal event. The spiritual and the physical, the divinity and its artistic image interpenetrate completely only in the period shortly preceding the earthly life of Christ in the Greek temple and in the classical Greek statue. In the periods before and after, art always points to a spiritual element beyond itself, either in the surrounding macrocosm or in the depth of the microcosm, man. Even for a non-Christian this process is well known. It is the characteristic path of a new idea through time. Gradually it penetrates the material substratum until it becomes completely absorbed and expressed in a perfect form. This state, however, cannot endure, because the form then begins to lead a life of its own, slowly becoming enriched and transformed until it points to something beyond the original intention in a more refined and individualized fashion. In Hegel's and Steiner's views of world evolution, here followed by Richter, the human being undergoes a vast learning process in which the spiritual forces of the cosmos are made more and more inward, are increasingly absorbed, until they become inner phenomena entirely individualized and shaped by man's own mind. Christ's incarnation, death, and resurrection make visible in explicit imagery this grandiose transforming path of the human being and his world. To make us experience this process in art is the intent of Richter's book. Like every great work it points beyond its subject, the history of art, into the universally human, and the Christianity it reflects moves beyond the narrow doctrines of any denomination or sect into the midst of man's religious experience in general.

Konrad Oberhuber
Harvard University

INTRODUCTION

The subtitle of the first edition of this book stated clearly what the thoughts it contains were meant to be: "Contributions to a History of Man."

Goethe once said that "the whole of mankind" can be regarded as "the true human being." This means that man is both a visible and an invisible being. What has become visible of him so far, in countless individuals and in the tremendous variety of nations and peoples, is but one stage of his development, an attempt by the invisible being that he actually is to realize "itself" in time and space. Just as, in this way, the human being unfolds "horizontally," so to speak, what appears in history is something like a "vertical" unfolding. World history is not only the sum of the histories of the individual peoples. It is the manifestation of precisely this visible-invisible human being who has been developing and struggling into existence step by step for thousands of years, in innumerable single individualities, within the nationalities and cultures that blossom and die away again. Nothing can be more interesting to man than this process, for it is our very own evolution. This process is by no means at an end; it continues on within ourselves, as this being continues its struggle to unfold.

This is a picture of the method employed in the present study. It is the same one Goethe developed, especially in his scientific studies, where he called it "contemplative observation" (*Anschauende Urteilskraft*). It consists of a continual striving not to think "about" the phenomena as such, but rather from within them, or out of them; in other words, to "perceive the idea within the reality."

This book is an attempt to read art history from such a point of view. It should be obvious that through the history of art the above-mentioned "vertical" evolution of man can become visible in a special way. For works of art are always a manifestation of the fact that an experience has been raised above the level of the merely personal into the sphere of the human being as such. This is why they contain within themselves the power to touch each one of us to a greater or lesser degree and to lift us up beyond our individual selves. Every work of art is a symbol, a hiero-glyph of a "human" experience.

The possibility of feeling deep reverence in the presence of works of art, quite independently of their content or their purpose, is a common experience. But the possibility of understanding history, especially art history, as the manifestation and working of a higher, spiritual entity would not exist for us without the Anthroposophy of Rudolf Steiner, to which the author owes his decisive points of departure.

The motto of the earlier editions of this book must be repeated here. As Paul Klee once said, "Art does not reproduce the visible, but makes visible." Similarly, the aim of this book is not to reproduce the whole of what is visible as art history, but rather to make something visible.

Ulm, Epiphany, 1976   Gottfried Richter

TRANSLATORS' COMMENTS

The original German title of Gottfried Richter's book is *Ideen zur Kunstgeschichte*, or *Reflections on Art History*. This title characterizes aptly the rather free, almost conversational tone of the German text and the informal, but often aphoristic and emphatic way in which many of the ideas are expressed.

Another prominent feature of the German text is the frequent and careful repetition of individual terms, phrases or whole sentences, often in the form of what the English reader might consider "plays on words." These leitmotifs have the effect of suddenly and startlingly linking widely separated parts of the text, and thus widely separated periods of art evolution, into a tremendous, dynamic mosaic.

The more thematic title chosen for the English edition focuses on the book's central idea, of which the artistic form of the text, like the art works it deals with, is itself an expression. In making the translation, the translators have continually tried to find a kind of English that would represent the poetic freedom, the dynamism and, above all, the musicality of the original—and still be English.

Special thanks are due to David Adams, Margaret De Ris, Rev. Diethart Jaehnig, Christopher Franceschelli, Kurt Luckner, Basil Collins, Uta Schaub and Mary Lynn Channer for their generous assistance with this translation, and to the many other friends as well who so willingly and selflessly gave advice and help in times of need.

Burley Channer, The University of Toledo
Margaret Frohlich

I

ON THE MEANING OF HISTORY

"The world of matter is the end of God's paths." This sentence was written by the profound Swabian thinker and theosophist, Oetinger, and it should stand at the beginning of every reflection on art. For it applies to every work of art, and no art is possible unless the fundamental feeling which this sentence expresses is present, even though this feeling may be alive only in the unconscious; the feeling, namely, that the world—including both mankind and human destiny—is a densification of something higher, the expression or the becoming visible of something invisible. This expression, however, has been falsified and obscured and is in need of restoration.

The real meaning and intention of every work of art is to exhibit this more complete densification in physical form. Whether a work of art consists of stone, wood, color, tone, word or whatever, its physical aspect is the end of a path, the condensation and embodiment of something invisible which has become visible in this process. The path began with an "experience." In a work of art truly worthy of the name, this "experience" always originates in the spiritual world; it is the artist's sense of being looked at by a divine being. For true art takes what is merely personal and raises it to the level of what is shared by all humanity. It places it into the wholeness of the world and allows it to speak back to us out of this wholeness, out of eternity.

This process, however, is one of growth, for as human beings we are always becoming. Our lives are, or should be, at least, a gradual awakening into ever broader and more comprehensive spheres of human awareness, into higher and higher heavens. The life work of an artist is his innermost biography.

Mankind as a whole is involved in this same type of growth, awakening again and again to new stages of inner experience. Each great civilization is a new beginning at ever new stages along the pathway that all

1

mankind is travelling toward the Self and its realization. We come from God and return again to God. And the history of art is the innermost biography of Man.

Man was never able to form a column as a living, breathing being until he had first experienced "column-ness" within himself as the impulse to stand erect and yet be ready to support others, or as a single being who felt like both an individual and an integral part of a greater being. This was not always the case. Only very late, after he had overcome much else, did he look with wonder into this landscape of experience.

Man's journey through the long ages and the different peoples and cultures of the world takes him from one experience and stage of consciousness to another. Nowhere are these stages of inner experience accidental or arbitrary. His journey follows the same laws as the serene growth of a flower, which sends out leaf after leaf, puts forth buds, opens blossoms and bears fruit, each in its own time and each containing its own irreplaceable, unsurpassable, eternal value.

What man feels like as a part of the world as a whole is expressed most basically in the way he builds a house. If the result is to be right in a higher sense, he must have an architectural perception of the right way to build, and this feeling comes from the fact that he dwells in the "housing" of his body. The way he is able to build a house depends entirely on how he experiences himself within this body. The house is the direct and most elementary representation of the experience of "bodily nature" in the broadest sense of the term.

In speaking of ancient times, however, we have to say "temple" instead of "house." For an individual's private home is of no importance yet, just as he himself still has no role as a private person, nor even a real existence. The only thing that exists in this higher sense is the body of the community as a whole, in the form of the tribe, the people or the city. The single individual has a part in the existence of this community only to the degree that he finds his individuality within it.

Another aspect of the temple is that, as the dwelling place of the god, it is intended to be an image of the spiritual world. This is the case, for example, in the Buddhist temples of India, and there is still a feeling for this in the cathedrals of the Middle Ages. This is not, however, a contradiction of what was said earlier, because in ancient times the world was experienced as an immense body, and the human body was felt to be

2

a microcosm in which the gods are active, the planets move along their orbits, the constellations are fixed and the elements interweave with each other. All parts of the earth correspond to some part of Ymir, the giant of the Germanic legend. The temple is the body of God, of the macrocosm and of the microcosm; for as an expression of how man feels and views the world and is aware of his own nature at any given stage of his development, it is more direct, and therefore more complete than any philosophy. One can see that the goal of man's age-long journey is *interior space*. He reaches it at the time of the Renaissance.

We can study the entire pre-Renaissance history of mankind without finding an interior space that is truly self-contained, has an inner balance and is created from the inside out. Neither the Gothic nor the Romanesque cathedral, nor the early Christian basilica, is built that way, nor are the Greek, the Egyptian or the Indian temple. This will be discussed in detail later on. There are preliminary stages, and here and there we can see it coming, but interior space was not really achieved until the beginning of modern times.

Now for the first time man enters the interior space within himself, finds himself there and awakes with an infinite, triumphant joy and feeling of strength to the experience of a self-sustaining individuality that acknowledges no law but its own and no limit but the one it sets itself.

He begins to create out of himself. The work that he creates is now his own personal "confession," as Goethe later called it. No longer is he an anonymous member or tool of some greater being that does its work through him. He himself emerges from his work; the artists of those days liked to say quite literally that he looks out at us from within it. He *is* his work, for he expresses his own personality through it. He creates space around himself and projects a whole world into it out of his own nature. The Form he thus surrounds himself with is a part of his own being because he comes toward himself out of these works and finds himself again within them.

This is what speaks in a determined way through the architecture of those times, creating spaces in which man does not lose himself, but "comes to" himself instead. These spaces emphasize the central importance of his being. They confirm his existence and enable him to experience himself in a stronger way. They do not point to something beyond themselves, but are at rest, enclosed within their own boundaries.

We will not really see the world-historical, or "cosmic," significance of what these artists accomplished until we go far back into the past and look at the very different historical counterpart which it presents.

The Chinese culture is the most ancient one we know. Externally its traditions can be traced back to the 4th millenium B.C., a period of considerable antiquity in itself. But we must realize that its actual roots reach back to a time many thousands of years earlier. In any case, there is much to be said for the idea that we are dealing here with a culture in which remnants of the ancient Atlantean consciousness are still at work, directly and essentially unchanged. For this entire culture speaks a language which is so alien to us, and is in fact so completely and fundamentally the opposite of everything we otherwise know, that its only possible point of origin lies on the other side of that great flood which we must speak of as the primordial boundary of all our modern cultures.

Again and again we find the Chinese house—the temple as well as the private home—built in the same peculiar way: all the surfaces of the roof are curved upwards toward the outside, like vessels held open to receive what comes toward them from heaven and the spiritual world. Often this effect is emphasized and enhanced by having several such roofs stacked one above the other (Plate 1).

This is the exact opposite of the picture we have before us in the architecture of the Renaissance. If we try to sense the form of such an ancient Chinese building with our own body, to take it into ourselves and let it mold us according to its will, we experience something which we moderns could hardly experience in any other way: the central point of this house, the center of gravity which supports it, is not in its interior at all, but outside it. In fact, there is not just one such central point, but several. This shows quite clearly how the people of that time felt about their world: that its creative center was to be sought in cosmic spaces outside the earth. This was where the earth had come from; from here it had received its forms and the laws of its existence. My law, the ancient Chinese felt, the force that shapes me, does not work into me but only approaches me from universal cosmic spaces. There is nothing independent about me at all. I am only, so to speak, "focussed into existence" by what is above and behind me. The "Son of Heaven" comes from outside

Plate 1. Chinese Temple.

4

the earth. As for the earth itself, until the beginning of our present century it was considered indecent to use the word "feet" in connection with it.

The divine home, that innermost space which man can go into with the help of his religion and feel at rest in, is outside. Those strange gates that stand all by themselves in the open Chinese landscape say the very same thing. As gates, they signify an "entrance" or a "threshold." But on the other side of these gates there is no temple. In fact, there is nothing at all that would suggest an interior space. There is only "world." They lead "into" the outside itself (Plate 2).

The ancestor cult of the Chinese (and once more we have to say: as it lived on until the beginning of our century) is also at home in this way of feeling about the world. Today we live for the child and for its sake. We have our eyes set on what we ourselves have given birth to and what will go on beyond us. The Chinese lived for the sake of his ancestors who had come before him, and children were important because they could carry on the ancestor cult and eventually include their own parents in their ancestral chain. The most important thing for him, his goal and his law, was thus not what he would give birth to out of himself, but rather that "other" out of which he himself had been born: the Not-I. And so, when someone would say jokingly that he had just come back from China "where people run around on their heads" (because they live on the other side of the earth), this picture contained a certain element of truth.

Now one should, of course, not say things like this for the sole reason that the roof of the Chinese temple has such a strange shape. But one could easily point out how the same law which led to this peculiar form in architecture was at work in all other manifestations of ancient Chinese culture. This architecture is simply, as it were, an incarnation, the direct architectural embodiment of the same archetype which found other forms in countless other metamorphoses throughout the entire culture. It was just as alive in ancient Chinese painting, the charm of which consists in the fact that it grasped the phenomena of the sense-world entirely from the outside, approaching them from some central point outside the human. One could also observe it in the sculpture, the poetry, the philosophy, the social laws and the customs.

Plate 2. Gate north of Peking on the way to the Ming Graves situated on the mountain slopes.

7

All this is an expression of what we have already referred to as the "Atlantean consciousness." On the basis of many different kinds of evidence we may assume today that long before the ancient Indians and Babylonians there was an ancient Atlantean culture. Spiritual science confirms and clarifies what historical and ethnological research has discovered.[1] At that time mankind must have had an entirely different consciousness. Traces of it can be found everywhere in legends and myths. It must have been a picture consciousness, hovering above the earthly, not rooted in intellectual thinking or in earthly matter as such.

The tremendous inner contrast between Chinese and Renaissance architecture is now becoming apparent. The architecture of the Renaissance is *the reverse* of what corresponds to the Atlantean consciousness (Plate 3). This powerful process of development starts with the new beginning of human culture after the great flood and goes on for thousands of years. This is the meaning of the new world-day into which mankind again awoke after the night into which the sun of Atlantis had set.

What this means may possibly become clearer if we try to understand the Chinese culture inversely by experiencing it as though we had turned ourselves inside out. We must really try to grasp this idea of turning ourselves inside out like a glove if we want to understand the essence of the Chinese point of view.

The importance of this cannot be overestimated, for it involves nothing less than our comprehension of the meaning of the whole development of the earth. The path from ancient Atlantis to modern times is not only the path toward the center or interior space of man, but also the one toward the inner space and center of the world: inside the earth itself.

One of the most impressive scenes from the time when man awoke so powerfully to an awareness of interior space and actually entered it was that event during the Imperial Diet in Worms when Luther—and who had he been until then, anyway?—stood up and declared in the face of the Pope, the Council, the bishops, the Emperor, the princes and everything else that until that moment had been regarded as an undisputed, divinely established authority, "Here I stand, I cannot do other-

Plate 3. Rome. Dome of St. Peter's. Completed in 1590 from designs by Raphael and Michelangelo.

wise, so help me God, Amen!" (Even if these were not his exact words, as many have argued, they were still the content of his inspiration.) There stood a man who had found within himself the center of the world in which God was speaking. How else could he have found the honest courage to speak out as he did? Today we can hardly grasp what that must have meant. What an unheard-of risk it was for a single man to regard the voice within his own breast as weightier and more binding than the power of an entire time-honored tradition. How agonizingly had a single man struggled with this idea for many years, and at this moment he was declaring by his action: God no longer speaks outside of us in a community tradition that has been handed down; today He speaks in the inner self of man. Man had found God within himself. This is the unprecedented importance of that moment.

Nowadays one would tend to say that this was the obvious consequence of man's finding himself within himself. But we could also conceive the greater reality that just the opposite had happened: namely, that man was able to find himself within himself because God had left His heavens, in which the ancient peoples had still found Him; He had come down to earth, had even been laid into the earth, and was now beginning to arise again out of man's own inner self. This process had required millennia to accomplish, beginning thousands of years before our era and needing thousands more beyond it for its completion.

We must learn to regard the Mystery of Golgotha as a cosmic event again and to listen to His steps as He goes on His way through past and future ages, for that, too, is a part of His new and mighty resurrection in our time.

This is what, one after another, the great civilizations of the past have shown us in their art more directly than in any other way: where and how they have found God within the wholeness of the world. They have found Him "on the way," as He strode from star to star, causing one region of the universe after another to glow with the brightness of His being, down to the darkest, but now the brightest, of all stars: the earth. Works of art are like the traces of His feet.

II

THE SUN-WORD

The Nature of Egyptian Art

Looking at the history of mankind, we can become aware of wonderful rhythms inherent in its overall grandiose development. At the same time we have to say that the high points and unsurpassable achievements of an individual cultural epoch give each such epoch its own unique and irrevocable character and value. One can say that being a man is somehow "more" than being a teenager, and being a teenager is "more" than being a young boy or a small child; yet each stage has an incomparable value of its own.

"Monumental" is a word that comes very close to expressing the basic characteristic of Egyptian art. Never before and never since has the quality of monumentality been achieved as fully as it was in Egypt. The reason for this is not the external size and massiveness of their works, although the Egyptians admittedly achieved some amazing things in this respect. Many modern structures surpass those of Egypt in terms of purely physical size. But massiveness has nothing to do with monumentality. An Egyptian sculpture no bigger than a person's hand is more monumental than that gigantic pile of stones that constitutes the war memorial in Leipzig, for instance. Monumentality is not a matter of external weight, but of "inner weight." This inner weight is the quality which Egyptian art possesses to such a degree that everything in it seems to be made of primeval stone, like a mountain range, even if it is only a few inches across or carved in wood. For no one has ever understood stone as well as the Egyptian: stone and its eternal silence. Stone, though, is not silent because it is empty but because its unspoken word is powerful beyond expression. In Franz Werfel's drama of St. Paul, the son, shaken with emotion as he looks at the corpse of his aged, wise and kind-hearted father, asks, "Father, why is your silence so powerful?" His question sounds as if it were coming from Egypt. Egypt is one single, powerful silence.

Architecture

Of all the architecture of ancient Egypt, the only buildings that have come down to us are hieratic ones: temples, pyramids and tombs. Not a single palace or private home is left now, although from excavations and plans and drawings that have been found we know very well what such buildings looked like. But this loss is not so significant if we realize that in Egypt, what men live in is not important; what matters is what the gods live in.

What does an Egyptian temple look like? What experience is its shape the "gesture" of, and what experience did it arouse in a person who went into it?

In those days, no one would enter the temple as a single individual, but would advance toward it in a long and solemn procession as part of a larger group. Incense would rise, songs would resound, and the clatter of sistra would intermingle with the songs and incense. By now the souls of those approaching the sanctuary were deeply stirred. The procession moved along a longer or shorter avenue lined with sphinxes which gazed down upon it from both sides with an indescribable expression. At the end of this avenue rose an enormous wall: the *pylon* of the temple. The eye had seen it already from a distance. To those who were moving toward it, it seemed to rise higher and higher, threatening, gigantic, overpoweringly super-human (Plate 4).

In its center is a portal, narrow, steep and inexorably stern. Gigantic stone figures stand on either side of it. But man must pass through it. The whole massive front of the temple is there for the sake of this one compelling gate.

How deeply shaken the people who stood there must have been. For

Plate 4. Edfu. Pylon of the Horus Temple.

12

the experience that the Egyptian temple addresses to those who approach it is this: they must first encounter a gigantic wall and then go through it, forcing their way into an interior that may well harbor enormous and entirely hidden dangers.

The Egyptian experiences how man enters his own house—how, coming from the outside, he is guided to its threshold. In those days the souls of men were still intensely absorbed in the outside world and the expanses of the heavens. These temples must have been a tremendous education toward self-awareness, guiding man into new and almost unbearable inner movements and experiences. The closer a man came to it, the more this wall pushed its way into him. Its gesture forced him deeper and deeper into his own physical body.

This is the Egyptian's archetypal experience. In fact, it may be called *the* architectural experience of Egypt. For thousands of years all Egyptian temples were built in exactly the same way. The layouts of the ones from the centuries just before the birth of Christ are essentially the same as the ones built around 1500 B.C. and earlier. (Much earlier, however, sometime before the 5th Dynasty, the laws of building that the great pyramid builders went by were in part exactly the opposite of the later ones. We will discuss this later, in dealing with the history of Egyptian art.) But there is another sense in which it can be said that this was *the* architectural experience. It comes again and again, each time more intensely, as one moves through the whole temple from space to space. One comes to wall after wall and has to break through it into a new interior. Each new space is narrower and lower than the last, each new doorway more contracted and more severe. What was first an infinite expanse changes more and more into an enclosing, oppressive closeness as one walks from portal to portal. Finally, in the lowest and narrowest of all the rooms, one may enter the holy of holies and stand face to face with the god himself (Plate 5).

The common people, of course, did not get to experience these repeated "enterings." They were allowed into the temple only as far as the great court behind the pylon that was open to the sky and surrounded by a colonnade. There they could see solemn sacrifices being made at the large

Plate 5. Edfu. Temple of Horus. Entrance halls and view into the sanctuary through the Hypostyle Hall with its typical plant-columns. Time of the Ptolemies.

15

Plate 6. Sakkara. False door with statues of the deceased inside the tomb of Nefer-Seshem-Ptah. About 2300 B.C.

altar and watch the smoke as it rose to the eternally blue sky. The emotional experience of going through the pylon must have been all they were able to bear as yet. Only the initiate who had strengthened his soul was allowed to go further, deeper and deeper "inside."

This temple-path along which he was guided is indeed a sacred one, for it is part of the path that for thousands of years *man* has been walking along toward himself. How secluded the interior of the actual temple was! There were no windows. A dim light came in only through openings in the roof. In these rooms the outer world and its light had ceased to exist. Moreover, around this windowless temple wall ran a second wall just as solid as the first one which created a narrow shaftlike passage around the temple.

But what we mainly find again and again is doors, doors that break through walls. And yet this "real" need does not seem to have been enough to satisfy the builders, who made false doors as well (Plate 6). This experience of the door and the sacred pathway was especially important for the construction of the countless tombs. In these, figures were sometimes even added to the false doors who seem to be coming through from the other side. Such doors are a clear indication that "portal," as a spiritual experience, was what mattered most.

Modern interpreters occasionally maintain that these false doors were built in order to deceive would-be tomb robbers. But this primitive explanation contradicts many of the facts, ignoring the most essential ones in the process. Works of art and religion are never concerned originally with some outward purpose but rather with the struggle to express inner experiences, to create a world in which inner and outer experiences are intimately and exactly interwoven.

This whole world of experiences can be characterized from another aspect as well; they are *experiences of waking up*. In his architecture the Egyptian shaped in stone what he experienced when in the morning he would come back from the world of night into the "enclosure" of his body. This is where man breaks through the wall; he steps out of the heavenly expanses of the cosmos and crosses the threshold into the narrow, disquieting house of his body. Man's experience in ancient Egypt was to wake up to his own earthly body. It would be more exact to say that man was actually just beginning to wake up, for he was still only crossing the threshold to the level of the dream. Struggling to wake up, he could not get beyond the border between two worlds.

Waking up, however, means standing up, and whoever stands up, wakes up. The Egyptian has given us an exact picture of this experience, or rather, he has shown us the pathway to the experience itself.

Our picture of the pylon and the way the Egyptian experienced it is not complete, however, until we add the fact that in front of the pylon there also stood an *obelisk*. Its form is related both outwardly and inwardly to the form of the pyramid, which had been worked out earlier. In fact, the obelisk even becomes a small pyramid at its upper end. But the inner law that leads to the one or the other form works in two different directions. The pyramid "grows" from above downward. Beginning at its apex, it radiates and widens downward into the spatiality of the earth, out of spacelessness into space. The obelisk, on the other hand, "grows" upward. Slim and steep, stretching toward heaven, it embodies the force of erectness (Fig. 1).

17

Fig. 1. Reconstruction of an Egyptian temple.

Added to this, along both sides of the avenue leading toward the pylon there was a row of crouching, sphinx-like animals who seemed to have fallen heavily to their knees. Whoever walked down that avenue was filled with the experience of the horizontal and of the deepest cosmic peace, completely immersed in this heavy crouching. Suddenly, out of all this horizontality, the obelisk juts up. We should try to re-experience the almost painful power of this contrast to get some idea of what it all meant. Man is beginning to stand erect. A power has moved into him, and through it he is beginning to feel his own inner being. As he stands up, he wakes up. This is the deep, mysterious, organic connection between the obelisk and the pylon. Standing erect is the same thing as breaking through the wall. The avenue of the sphinxes with its obelisk and the huge wall of the pylon with its narrow, disquieting doorway are simply different aspects of the same experience (Plate 7). They seem like some dramatic mystery rite that has been fixed in stone, "Feel the power of uprightness—the power of your own ego-being—drawing into you . . . and you will awaken!"

After this comes the experience of the Egyptian *column*. The Great Court is surrounded by them, and eventually it extends into a forest of columns which constitutes the hypostyle, or "Hall of Columns" itself. Here one sees more clearly than anywhere else that in this early stage of waking up the Egyptian still experiences this awakening more as a dream than as actual awakeness. He is still only standing at the threshold.

Some people have tried to explain the peculiar form of the Egyptian

18

Plate 7. Karnak. Avenue of the Sphinxes, leading from the Nile to the temple of Amon. Built by Ramesses II (1290-1223 B.C.).

column as stone imitations of bundles of lotus or papyrus stems that had originally been bound around the top of a wooden pole. This may well have been the external model, but it completely misses the essential point. The real question is why these particular plant forms were chosen at all and why they made such a strong impression that they remained unchanged for thousands of years. Such forms, if arbitrary, could easily have given way to others that were just as accidental in origin. How are principles like these supposed to explain the Hathor-column, whose capitals depict the head of Hathor, the great goddess of heaven, crowned with cow horns? Such "explanations" only shift the problem back one step. In the end there is nothing to do but look for the origin of the form in the original artistic experience itself.

What are they really, these enormous, plantlike "growths": the colossal shafts of the columns with their dizzying heights; these structures so far beyond all human measure that they make man feel as small as he would feel in the face of unleashed forces of nature; and finally, the strange shape of the capitals themselves with their forms that swell like buds or sprout like blossoms? If we try to make all this alive and give it some shape again within ourselves, listening all the while to whatever sensations it calls up within us, we eventually come to experiences very much like the ones we still have sometimes in feverish dreams, when we are lifted out of our normal consciousness a little and find ourselves standing at the threshold. At such moments we experience, if only in their pathological variant, the swelling, surging forces of the "etheric body," the forces of growth and of vegetative plant life which are the real builders of our physical body.[2]

These forces are what the Egyptian was actually depicting in his columns. When the human being enters the "house" of his body, the first thing he meets with there is the working of his etheric body. The Egyptian still experienced this so strongly because he had not yet awakened fully into a daytime consciousness; he was still just at that border where dream and day intermingle. He was actually depicting such "vegetative growth" in his columns, but not for festive decoration or mere "embellishment." Nor was he imitating the external form of any kind of plant, but rather "plantness" itself, as he could still experience it within his own being. The pylon and the solid temple wall enabled him to re-experience in them his own body in terms of its physical firmness and the way it furthered his sense of individuality by separating him off from the rest of his environment. In the same way, he could re-experience in these columns the forces that creatively built up and shaped that body.

This is the only way to understand the organic aspect of the *Hathor capital* as well (Plate 8).

Hathor, whose name means "House of Horus", is depicted as having a human face and the horns and ears of a cow, but frequently she is portrayed directly as a cow. She is the great goddess of heaven and probably one of the most ancient divinities of Egypt. What animal could be a stronger and more elemental symbol of the working of the vegetative forces than this one? As she lies on the meadow chewing her cud, or licking her calf and giving it milk, completely given over to the blissful en-

Plate 8. Hathor capitals in the ante-room of the Temple of Hathor in Dendera. 1st century B.C.

joyment of all the life processes that are flowing through her, the cow is something like a cosmic "symbol." This is why she has always been a sacred animal in India, where the whole culture was essentially a culture of the etheric body. It is also why her face appeares on the Egyptian columns by a kind of inner necessity.

One could say that Hathor's countenance looked out at the Egyptian from the etheric world, directly and as a matter of course. Meeting her there was no different from experiencing the forms of the plants themselves rising and swelling up in front of him.

For in the whole living world around him he was still able to experience the mighty, superhuman forces of the cosmos. He felt his body permeated by Powers whose presence made his existence seem utterly insignificant. Their grandeur inspired him with both awe and terror. In them he heard the mighty voice of God.

Sculpture

What do we see when we observe how the Egyptian went about reproducing the human body itself in his sculptures?

In the earlier period two or three basic types of figures predominate, sitting ones and standing or striding ones. Let us consider the sitting ones first.

To begin with, they sit solemnly on thrones. They hold the upper part of their bodies firmly erect, and the severity of this posture is intensified by the way they hold their heads. One arm lies at a right angle across the chest while the other one rests horizontally on the upper thigh, all the way to the open palm. Sometimes both arms lie along this line. There are nothing but horizontals and verticals in the whole statue. The tension inherent in the three dimensions of space has been lived through and depicted here with a decisiveness that reminds us of systems of crystals. We are awed, however, by the enigmatic expressions of the faces that gaze awesomely into a distance which we are at a loss even to look for at first. It is that terrifying distance beyond all finite limits (Plate 9).

Plate 9. Statue of King Khephren. Green diorite. From the Temple of the Dead in front of the pyramid in Giza. 4th dynasty. Cairo Museum.

The austerity which has nearly rigidified these figures is not, however, a sign of death. A tremendous life and inner movement fills them to their outermost limits, but all this they keep to themselves. What we have said about Egypt's being one great silence is more evident in these figures than anywhere else. And yet, in them the silence has become so great that we can almost hear it again, revealing its secrets.

For what these figures relentlessly keep from passing beyond the strict boundaries of their being becomes just that much more powerful *within* them. Words, murmured by ancient gods in primeval times, melodies that no instrument can reproduce: these whisper, rise, fall and circulate throughout their being, behind their silence . . .

We can only understand their enigmatic nature by looking at the other basic type of statuary, the *striding figures* (Plate 10).

How they stride, as though from one eternity to another! Their walking absorbs them so completely that the only reality they know is the overwhelming grip of a higher guidance. They seem like beings who go from star to star, for the earth has no spaces like the ones in which they live and move. The soles of their feet know nothing of the ground on which they stand. The knees, the hips, indeed the whole of the striding body has no sense of itself at all; it senses only the overpowering command that it must obey. Of all earthly creatures, only the animals walk like this. Their gait has something of this "unquestioning obedience to a higher law" about it. They obey this law just as flowing water obeys the one that belongs to it.

Such a comparison is much more than a simple allegory. Deep down within its nature the Egyptian culture had a mysterious relationship to the world of animals. The fact that nearly all Egyptian gods have animal heads, or are even experienced in the form of animals at all, has its origin in this level of the Egyptian character.

In this connection, however, being an animal does not mean being something "lower" than a human being. What was said at the beginning of this chapter is also true here, that every stage of existence has its own irreversible value within itself.

What is really going on here?

Man was not always a human being. Slowly, in wonderful stages and

Plate 10. Perhernofret. Wood, originally covered with stucco. 5th dynasty. Berlin.

25

rhythms, he has developed through all the stages of existence toward himself. Having passed through the various stages of stone, plant and animal, he now carries all these as what we might call "cosmic memories" within himself. On the one hand, such "development toward himself" has been a steady evolution and a continuous gain. On the other hand, at least for the time being it has also been an irrecoverable loss, in that step by step he has slipped farther and farther down out of the cosmic orders of existence. The result has been a loss of cosmic consciousness.

What, then, does it mean when the Egyptian represents the gods and the animals as beings of a kindred nature? Nothing less than his strange, deep memory of a stage of existence when man still lived within the cosmic order. It was an "ancestor cult," if we may call it that; as such, it was the most wonderful ancestor cult that ever existed, for it reached back into an inconceivable past beyond all human calculation.[3] We should also keep this in mind when we look at Egyptian animal sculpture. For the Egyptian, animal existence meant, more than anything else, elemental existence, obeying the Great Law and thus being innocent in the deepest sense of the word and always right, in harmony with the cosmos.

This is the secret of the Egyptian gods and the secret of the striding figures. They speak of buried memories: divine animal existence slumbering within them, cosmic spaces, awareness of the gods and mysteries of stars. Deep within them something is stirring.

This stirring still reverberates in the sitting figures. These figures have only come to rest in an outward sense, for the melody of their walking is still very much alive within them. They are still completely absorbed in it, only now in a different way. As striding figures they followed it with their whole body; now, their body is fixed, and they can only follow it as listeners. But they listen with their entire being to what is happening within themselves. Sometimes—like Nature, who always reveals her secret at some point or other—they too betray the melody of their walking, which they can hear but normally keep so powerfully silent.

There is an ancient statue of *Khephren*, the builder of one of the great pyramids. From the front nothing seems unusual about it. But from the side we see a falcon sitting bolt upright behind the king's head, embrac-

Plate 11. King Khephren with Horus-falcon. Detail, side view of Plate 9.

ing it with outstretched wings and directing its stern gaze down at him. This is the Horus-falcon, the symbol of the sun god. Protecting, embracing, inspiring, it sits there, giving something of its own nature to the king. A half ironic, half painful smile plays gently around the Pharaoh's mouth. It is the smile of a Knower; the smile of a god radiating down over all mankind (Plate 11).

For Khephren hears—actually hears!—what a great poet would express in a different way thousands of years later,

> "The sun resounds, in ancient fashion
> in wager-song of brother spheres . . ."
> (Goethe's *Faust*)

He hears the ancient words of creation which have given rise to all that is; he hears them as though they were resounding out of the heart of the world itself.

The sun has many names and shapes because it works in many ways. One of the chief names of the sun god is Re. In hieroglyphs it is written like this: ⊙ ◡ .

The second of these signs, and in this case the most important one, is a mouth. Written as ◡ it means both "mouth" and "the word." *RE* as a verb means "to create existence." To experience the sun therefore means to experience "the WORD," which, as the harmony of the spheres, rules throughout the world, creating existence. This is the mighty secret that the Egyptian statues keep so powerfully silent, for it is what Egypt heard when it entered the body of earth and awakened to it.

Myth

At this point we need to deal briefly with the content of Egyptian consciousness.

This consciousness is still entirely mythical. The later philosophers' ability to form clearly delineated concepts is not yet one of its characteristics. The Egyptian still "dreams" his world in wonderful pictures, but these pictures contain a wisdom that is deep and infinitely great. Of course, the modern mind sees in them one enigma after another, for the laws of mythical and of logical consciousness are completely different. Mythical consciousness, for example, is absolutely unable to create a "system" of thought, a canon, or a dogma. There is as yet no need for it to prove the unity of the world to itself in some abstract way. Things stand side by side in it that seem completely contradictory to modern thinkers, and as a way of thinking, it often enough drives such thinkers to despair.

The simplest way to differentiate intellectual from mythical consciousness is to say that they use two different kinds of language. The language of mythical consciousness comes from a different realm of existence and has to be "translated" out of this realm just like any other language. The trouble is, we have no dictionaries to help us. Like any living thing, each image in this language can have many facets and many different "meanings," depending on its context. Even so, it has the same definite limitations as any other piece of reality, since the language of this imagery was created from reality—a reality, however, which the Egyptians felt to be richly interwoven with a spiritual element. For them the things of this world were not as bare and harshly unrelated as they seem to us today. They were all interwoven, and everything was constantly changing into something else. Life expressed itself in many interrelated ways, and the Egyptians sensed the drama and the destiny of each such expression as an integral part of the phenomena themselves. They did not grasp the phenomena of the physical sense-world as dead abstractions yet, but were still able to experience them deeply within the dramatic context of the whole of life. The laws that govern a consciousness of this sort stem from what is organic and alive (in other words, etheric), just as the laws that govern intellectual consciousness belong to what is mechanical and dead, or physical.

Now it would be foolish to assume, for example, that the ancient Egyptian actually regarded the Apis bull which he took care of in his temple and sometimes led around through the countryside in a solemn procession, as a god. One could well say, however, that he experienced the being or the "soul" of a god as it revealed itself through the bull while resting on its back. (This real image did not fade away until a later period of cultural decline.) For the Egyptian the tremendous procreative power of the bull was a manifestation of the creative power in the world as a whole. For this reason he said that "the soul of Ptah" rested on Apis's back. Ptah, however, is "the creator of all creators, the potter of all potters"; he is the "father of all the gods, the Great God of the Very Beginning who existed before all others."

Ptah is also called "the Lord of the Cool Water," a strange designation that hardly seems related to his other names at first. But we begin to understand it when we come to see more in the word "water" than the mere name of a chemical formula. To the Egyptian, "water" meant the whole sphere of fertile etheric life, the bridge which everything spiritual must cross on its way into physical incarnation. This is why he spoke of the "cool water . . . under the body of the Goddess of Heaven." The spirit of God moves upon the face of the waters, even yet.

This is why Ptah was also the "Lord of the Master Craftsmen." They were his priests, and it was their job to make his essence manifest. In Memphis, where the cult of the Apis bull was especially strong, the high priest of the sanctuary was called the "Head of the Master Craftsmen," just as the high priest of Heliopolis, the city of the sun, bore the name, "The One Great in Vision."

We mentioned earlier that the Egyptian religion was not organized into a coherent system. It also had no holy book or canonical writings, such as the Koran or the Bible. Each temple school developed its own theology according to the special position which it occupied within the whole organic structure. The world of the healer is different from that of the artist, the soldier, the judge or the scribe. As an organism, the world is a symphony of the most diverse elements. Canons and dogmas are unnecessary if the world itself is still an undivided whole and each thing in it a hieroglyph or a holy rune of God, mysterious, but legible to one who knows.

One temple school, however, systematized its knowledge more than the others: the school of Heliopolis. As its name indicates, it was a sanctuary to the sun and for just this reason it most probably administered certain mysteries of central importance. Among the various mystery centers it may well have been regarded as a kind of heart-being, to and from which the homogeneous, living blood flowed that pulsated through the organism's other members as well.

In this sanctuary the teaching known as "the great ninefoldness of Heliopolis" was developed. This teaching is a sort of genealogical history of the gods that would look something like this if stated in the form of an abbreviated chart:

<pre>
                    Ptah
            Shu   Tefnet
        Geb   Nut
    Osiris   Isis   Set   Nephthys
</pre>

All nine of these together are called Atum, the Sun God, whose other name is Re.

This is a very important fact, for if we translate it into the language of modern consciousness it means that the entire divine organism of the world—by which we mean that world, within and behind the world of the senses, that is actually made up of creative spiritual beings—is completely permeated and ruled by the power of the divine "Word."

In his own way the Egyptian was saying the same thing here that John the Evangelist would say thousands of years later in the prologue of his gospel, "In the beginning was *the Word,* and *the Word* was with God, and *the Word* was God. The same was in the beginning with God. All things were made by him; and without him was not any thing made that was made. In him was life; and the life was the light of men."

For the Egyptian the world is the great self-expression of God. The sacred Word of its primal creator whispers through it. This whisper is what the Egyptian and his statues are both listening to, and as a result the whole of Egyptian life is still a religious service. All its activity is priestly: the artists are priests of Ptah, the physicians are priests of Sekhmet, the scribes are priests of Thoth and the judges are priests of the truth. Even the government officials are priests, for the entire state is organized hieratically. The physician causes forces of a cosmic order to stream into what has become dis-order in order to heal it; the judge works in harmony with the ancient, sacred law inherent in the world and in each of its creatures, to take what is no longer right and make it right again; the artist allows the creative forces of the spirit to stream into earthly substance. Each of these is a servant of the archetypal Word which permeates the world with its wise rule. Their professions and the whole of their activity are a constant prayer in its deepest and truest sense. All Egypt is filled with the whisper of this prayer, and in its temples and statues the stone itself learns to pray in words that cannot be spoken.

The pharaoh is not only the highest of the priests; he is a god as well, and as such he moves among the gods. We should take the Egyptians very seriously on this point, for they proclaimed it thousands of times in words and pictures. No lie could exist for 3000 years, demanding and receiving a millionfold sacrifice of life and strength from hundreds of thousands of people. Whatever has such power must contain truth as well. The pharaohs, who had actually experienced death and resurrection in the mysteries, had made their way to the divine foundations of the world. Again and again they had died under the awesome power of these experiences and had come forth from them again reborn. The pharaoh thus had every right to call each god his father and each goddess his mother. But the greatest of all his experiences may well have been to actually go through what was portrayed countless times in the image of the pharaoh's name that was inscribed by the gods in the tree of life. Every human being is a word that God himself has spoken, and God means something with every word He speaks. In a name this word can be heard, and the pharaoh who has passed through the initiation knows: Now the "Word" that I am is sounding; my whole inner being now resounds with the rustling of the Tree of the World, and the forces of divine life now flow through it, as was meant to be from the very beginning.

This knowledge of the sacred, primeval Word takes form once more in the grandiose image of Apis, the sacred bull, who is often shown carrying the sun between its horns. We dealt with this image earlier, but at this point we need to consider it again within a different context.

No two springtimes are alike. The spring sun shines down today from a different constellation than it did at the time of the ancient Greek, Egyptian, Persian and Indian civilizations. The point where the sun is located at the spring equinox travels from one constellation to another every 2,160 years. Wherever people understood these deeper connections, they also knew it was not a matter of indifference which sign of the zodiac a given culture was under. Egypt was under the sign of the bull, and this fact had a specific meaning. It was felt that the forces at work in individual human beings come from cosmic forces, as microcosm and macrocosm correspond. In particular, the power of speech was ascribed to the forces experienced in connection with the sign of the bull.

The Egyptian could still experience the power of procreation and the power of speech as one and the same thing. (The change of voice at puberty confirms the reality of this underlying connection.) Ptah, the god of creation, whose soul was said to be resting on Apis's back, is deeply bound up with the essential nature of the WORD.

The bull carries the sun through Egypt: this picture was re-enacted countless times in solemn processions, but it was only an external symbol of the cosmic situation which was being lived through inwardly. The creative energy that has brought *everything* into being is in the WORD. Egypt is a cosmic event.

But our description of the nature of Egyptian art and its impact on the history of mankind would be incomplete if we did not also add the following.

There is a quality of destiny which is truly awesome in the rapt listening of the motionless pharaohs seated on their thrones. These statues are a manifestation of what Rudolf Steiner once spoke of as the ability to sense the working of the stars and of cosmic forces in one's very body which some people in the Egyptian period still possessed. To do this, however, they had to remain absolutely still. Perhaps these figures affect us so deeply just because they are surrounded by the breath of this awesome destiny. They are still just barely able to hear the divine word. But how long will this be the case? How much longer will they be able to endure having such complete control over their every movement? For they understand with merciless clarity that a strong desire is already stirring in them to be someone on their own, separate from everything else. This desire wants to scatter their concentrated energy out into the world. Already they need a great deal of strength to maintain their concentration. How much longer can they go on?

The Egyptian statues are the signs of a time that it was our destiny to take leave of so long ago that today hardly anyone can know how far away it actually is. We would have to travel a long way with our imagination to find that distant point within ourselves where those ancient figures stand (Fig. 2).

This truth was cast into a gripping *myth* that must have been deeply rooted in the Egyptian unconscious, since we find it depicted so often in Egyptian art.

In ancient times, so the myth goes, the gods ruled on the earth itself. They had their homes here and went about on our streets and roads. Nut, the goddess of the sky, still rested on the body of Geb, the god of earth. One day it happened that the men of earth arose in a great revolt. Filled with wrath, the lion-headed Sekhmet went out after them, and even though, when they saw her, men turned pale and fled into the wilderness in terror, she destroyed so many of them that Re was afraid she would kill them all. But this he did not want, for they had been born from his own tears. And so he had an intoxicating red drink poured out in a great flood over all the earth. When Sekhmet arose the next morning

33

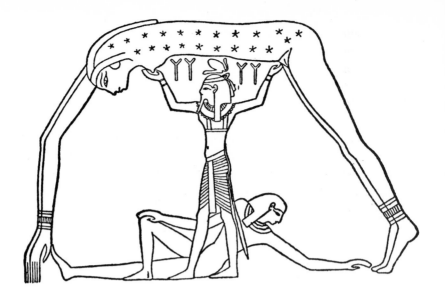

Fig. 2. Geb and Nut. The symbols underneath the body of the goddess of heaven signify the four "supports of heaven."

to finish off her work, the red flood deceived her. Seeing her own face reflected in it, she thought that it was blood and went back home to Re. But by this time Re was old and tired; "his bones were silver, his limbs had turned to gold and his hair to genuine lapis lazuli." And so he ordered Nut, the goddess of the sky, to get up off of Geb and Shu, her father, the god of the air, to be her support. With that, the sky rose up above the earth; and since that time the gods have had new paths of their own to travel on in those high spaces where the sun boat, the moon boat and all the stars now move as well. In the meantime, Re himself no longer rules, having transferred his regency to Thoth, the lord of the moon.

What does this myth mean in the language of modern consciousness? That once there was a time when the speech of the gods could be heard in everything that existed on the earth. The heavenly and the earthly, spirit and matter, were not yet split apart. Man could still feel archetypal divine powers at work in the very core of his being. This is how it was until man himself revolted by becoming a self-willed being, standing erect and refusing to simply submit any longer to the guidance of cosmic

34

forces streaming through him. At that point a new power appeared that had such a terrible effect on men that death became a mighty force among them and they had to flee to an exhausted, barren wasteland of desperation. Who is this power?

Sekhmet is the goddess of both war and the art of healing. The very peculiarity of this combination makes it evident who she really is and where she can be experienced, namely, in the "astral" or "soul body"[4] of man. The warrior lives in the surging emotions of this "soul body," but all illnesses have their origin in it too. This insight was the foundation of the entire Egyptian art of healing, and modern medicine is painstakingly finding its way back to it. This is also why Sekhmet was experienced as having the head of a lion, for the lion is an image of the astral in the same way as the cow is an image of the etheric.

Here, then, in the region of the soul, the power of the divine world has become so frightening that the Egyptian has to run away from it. Otherwise it will destroy him, because his egotism has alienated his soul from the godhead. That the "Red Sea" should then bring salvation is only an illusion; as yet this sea is really only the "sea" of the blood in which the new power of the ego is stirring. (In reality this is a gentle premonition of what is depicted later in the Bible with a much greater sense of finality as the destruction of the Egyptians during the safe passage of the Israelites across the Red Sea.) Now this sea surges up in a mighty flood, but it is no longer transparent. It works like a mirror, separating gods and men.

Heaven and the gods are far away now. But the most frightening thing is that Re, too, is gone. The sun-word no longer speaks directly and in an elemental way to the forces of the heart. As Re withdraws, only Thoth is left behind to rule: Thoth, the lord of the cold and rigid moon, who can only reflect light from the sun since he has none of his own. The forces of the isolated intellect are beginning to develop. Thoth is the god of the scribes, the judges and the mathematicians . . .

Such is the Egyptian myth of the Fall of Man out of the divine world order into the depths of his own individualized selfhood, where he now finds death.

We see in this the twofold aspect of Egyptian civilization: on the one hand, the desperate desire to cling to its magnificent mythical consciousness; on the other, the unconditional resolve to be a part of the earth and to wake up in the earthly body. There is something grandiose about the way in which the Egyptian goes consciously into a world of death. There is no doubt that the initiates, at least, who were the leaders of their people, knew what was going on. Otherwise they would never have practiced the mummy cult, that urge to possess an earthly body on beyond the point of death. Nor would they have erected towering pyramids or given the pylon of the temple its characteristic form. For all these things are only expressions of their desire for an earthly body and of their knowledge of death: even *the pylon* of the temple.

People have been speculating for a long time about the origin of the pylon's form. But in the end they have all had to admit that they had no idea where it came from, because they were always trying to derive the sacred from the profane and the spiritual from what is earthly. Egypt can never be understood this way. Nevertheless, in this particular instance the physical archetype of the pylon is known and there are thousands of examples of it.

The earliest evidence of "primitive" (if we insist on calling it that) three-dimensional construction in Egypt is the mastaba, or tomb. Its form is typical of the kind that most graves have today.

If we now imagine the mastaba growing taller without increasing the surface area of its base, we arrive at the form of the pylon. It is nothing but a mastaba stretched upwards: a menacing, towering tomb.

This is the wall that one comes up against, the gate that has to be passed through. *To enter the body means to enter the tomb.*

Finally, we come to the *pyramids,* which we will say more about in the following chapter. In his excellent book, *Die ägyptischen Pyramiden als Zeugen vergangener Mysterienweisheit (The Egyptian Pyramids as Tokens of Ancient Mystery Wisdom),*[5] Ernst Bindel has shown that their form can be derived genetically from that of the mastaba as well. At any rate, the Step Pyramid of Sakkara, which is the oldest of the great pyramids, still has a rectangular ground plan and resembles more than anything else a series of smaller and smaller mastabas stacked one on top of the other, as far as its overall form is concerned.

In its finished form, however, the pyramid is a gigantic, glistening crystal. This is how we should imagine the way it originally looked. Its whole surface was covered with slabs of polished limestone that were put together with such precision that even today a knife blade will not fit between any two of the slabs that are still preserved. It must have been difficult to look at the pyramid for very long; it was a veritable crystal, glittering brilliantly in the radiant Egyptian sun.

This crystalline quality of the pyramids has to be felt, as well as the mathematical quality of their physical structure and the character of their stone. For this huge crystal is a tomb. Whether the pyramids were originally built as burial places or for other purposes entirely is a question we may leave open for the time being. In either case they stand for an experience of death that was based on an exact, one-to-one correspondence with every aspect of the existence of an earthly body.

In one direction, then, the mastaba becomes the pylon; in another it becomes the pyramid, and the obelisk develops out of this. As the basis of the whole Egyptian experience we see the great Silence of the tomb emerging. The world has become an enormous tomb, grown silent now. And man, born of this world, cries out in awe-struck fear, "Father, why is your silence so powerful?"[6]

Babylon

Egypt's importance for humanity, as well as the uniqueness of the Egyptian achievement itself—which one is tempted to call its "historic deed"—shine out even more brightly against the background of contemporary cultural developments in Mesopotamia. In many respects the cultures of Sumer, Babylonia and Assyria can be grouped together as a single cultural unit.

The situations of these two civilizations were identical in terms of humanity's historical development. They both "expressed themselves" in forms which seem to be very much alike at first. But a closer look shows that their apparent similarity is actually a polarity (Fig. 3).

The most overpowering buildings which the Mesopotamian countries have produced and handed down to posterity are the *ziggurats*, even though today they are hardly more than crumbling ruins. These were sanctuaries built in the form of ascending steps. The biggest one was probably not as tall as the Pyramid of Cheops, but it was much taller than the pyramid of Mycerinus. It may seem grotesque to us today that the first person who went at these huge hills of debris to extricate their secrets attacked them with pick and crowbar in search of an interior in them that was simply not there. They did, of course, look something like the pyramids, which were already known and admired for the

37

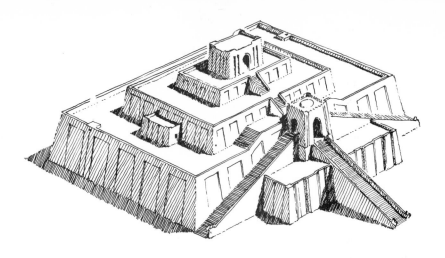

Fig. 3. Ziggurat of Urnammu at Ur. Reconstruction. The stairs along the sides are processional paths. The central flight of stairs was used only by the god as he descended from the "nuptial house" situated on the uppermost step.

mysterious and fabulous treasures which they contained, but that was all he could see in them. He had no way of knowing that by their very nature they were as different from the Egyptian pyramid as they could possibly be.

Inside its shining smoothness, the Egyptian pyramid closes itself off entirely from the outside world. It conceals its mysterious life in deeply hidden, inaccessible corridors and chambers and seems to be making a tremendous effort for the sake of a few relatively unimportant little rooms. With the ziggurat all this is exactly reversed. The stairs, which lead upward on the outside from one level to the next, have taken over the role of the corridors; that of the funerary chambers has been taken over by the small sanctuary on the uppermost platform of the ziggurat, where the holy meal and the "marriage" with the deity were celebrated. The ziggurat was built for what would take place on its outer surface.

The *gate*, too, plays just as important a role in Mesopotamia as it does in Egypt and is also experienced in exactly the opposite way. Whoever came toward the gate of the Egyptian temple felt pulled into it, and the false doors inside the tombs indicated the threshold across which someone had stepped into a hidden chamber. The Babylonian and Assyrian gates turn outward just as decisively as the Egyptian ones turn inward.

Whoever approaches them is overwhelmed by a stream of powerful, boundless life, expressed by endless processions of lions, bulls and mythical animals. This was a severe test for the pious to meet and pass; the unholy may well have failed it.

The gates of Egypt and of Mesopotamia are mirror images of each other. In Egypt, the gate leads into the body and the world of death. In Mesopotamia it is the door of heaven and of birth. Egypt's path is a sacred one that leads into the earth. In Assur and Babylon one seeks the path back up into the heavens, which are the source of all life and evolution. This is why Mesopotamia is filled with mythical creatures of the strangest sorts, and also why its gods have huge wings that allow them to float down to earthly men, bestow their gifts of blessings and fertility upon them and lift themselves back up again into their own kingdom.

When we now find that the mighty gates which justifiably moved their discoverers to amazement and admiration protected not only temples but whole cities as well, we see that the same thing is true for them. It makes no sense to regard them as nothing but fortifications in the modern sense. At most they would be this in the sense that their very impressiveness would show an approaching enemy how powerful the god or goddess dwelling in that particular city was. For the gods of this land are no mere companions of some lonely pharaoh's incarnation, but gods of the people. They love life and give mankind their gifts of law and justice. Hammurabi, long famous as the first great author of a code of justice, was at home in Babylon. Three centuries earlier his great predecessor, Lipit Ishtar of Nippur, had already had the first tablets inscribed which contained laws to protect the weak from the strong and the good from the bad. It was about this time that the "Precept for King Meri-ka-Re" came into existence in Egypt. Its advice is to be just, not for the sake of justice and to help the poor, but for the sake of having a good life after death[7] (Fig. 4).

The cultures of both Egypt and Mesopotamia stand at a threshold where the world of the gods is growing dim. It is still within man's reach, but has already become a world "other" than his own. At the same threshold those cultures are also beginning to sense the bitterness of death. This is the message of the powerful epic of Gilgamesh, whose friend, called back again as a spirit from the realm of the dead, says to him, "If I tell you the law of the earth which I have seen, you will sit down and weep." The land between the two rivers turns away with a

Fig. 4. Gate of Ishtar in Babylon. Reconstruction. The entire face of the gate and the frieze with the striding lions on the walls of the processional path were made of shiny glazed bricks. The background was dark blue, the animals yellow.

shudder and seeks its gods in the far reaches of the world before man's birth. Egypt, however, with superhuman courage, knocks at the door of death and enters—and there it finds its gods. From this moment on, everyone, even the harp-players and dancers, is pierced with the austere and bitter taste of death. But this is Egypt's greatness: that it so firmly resolved to follow the sacred temple pathway of humanity.

The Sphinx

There is still one more figure to discuss which was elaborated in Egypt and always appears in connection with the pyramids, namely, the sphinx. Its nature can be described from several different viewpoints. When we first look at it we see the body of an animal with a human head emerging from it. This picture is clearly related to those images of the Egyptian divinities that are depicted either in the form of human bodies with animal heads or simply as animals. We must see the sphinx in this context of man's struggle to free himself from his animal nature. But we must keep in mind that at the same time this animal nature was felt to be something divine. While the sphinx's animal body lies heavily outstretched in the horizontal plane, its human head stands bolt upright. We have the same contrast experienced and represented here which we studied earlier in connection with the obelisk. What does it mean to be human? It means to feel the power of the ego, the force that enables us to stand upright, living within us. Egypt does not experience *uprightness* in all its fullness yet, but only the fact that man is born into earthly existence in the process of *becoming upright*. In this sense Egypt stands at the threshold, and the sphinx is a threshold experience (Plate 12).

This enigmatic figure can be illuminated from another point of view as well. When the animal body that its human head is struggling to escape from is fully represented, it is made up of three different elements. The bull's body has the chest of a lion and powerful wings growing out of its sides. We can see from several things that have been mentioned already what this peculiar composition points to. It was a reproduction of what the Egyptian regarded as the whole human being. We have already spoken of the bull or cow as an image of the etheric and have at least touched on the relationship of the lion to the astral. The birdlike element, however—and for the moment it makes no difference whether the eagle or the falcon is taken as an image of this—stands for the highest member of man's being. The birdlike element soars high in the air; then it attacks sharply, swooping down to the earth from dizzying heights as if measuring out the whole space between heaven and earth and portraying in this way the powerful tension between these two poles. This element was always present wherever people thought in mythical pictures and was felt to be an image of everything connected with the human ego. The human element then represents what has actually become physical.

This, then, is the sphinx, whose very configuration has always seemed to be such a tremendous mystery. We find it resting in front of the pyramid, the mighty grave of the sun. In it the whole mysterious being of Egypt has taken on physical form. It conceals a word that man is supposed to know, but no longer does; a word that became mute when it entered his being.

Thousands of years later we see this image emerge again, but now, of course, it has a different form. Both in the early Christian centuries and

later on in medieval works of art, the eagle, the lion, the bull and the human being crop up again and again. But now when they appear they are either writing something or inspiring other people to write. They no longer keep the Word silent; they have become its proclaimers. In their midst we see the One whom John proclaimed as the WORD become flesh, enthroned and surrounded by a wreath of radiant light beams like the sun. This is where the resurrection of the WORD begins, but things will not be this way until much, much later. Egypt experiences the first beginnings of its death and entombment. For what occurred on the earth at the beginning of our era was only the end, the full-fillment, of a process which had begun thousands of years earlier.

At the same time it was the beginning of a process which will go on for thousands of years to come and in which we ourselves are still living: the resurrection of the WORD which once resounded from the sun down to the earth and into man.

But perhaps there was a hint or a prophecy of this resurrection already in Egypt, the land that bore the mystery of death so deeply within itself. If we assume that the pylon is really the mastaba, or the grave, stretched upwards, the question then arises: What is the meaning of the indentation in the middle of the upper edge of the pylon, over the portal? One could possibly explain it on the basis of a peculiar optical phenomenon. One has the impression that during a sunrise the horizon line is broken or indented at just that point where the sun appears. At the very same point on the pylon a representation actually appears of Khepri, the beetle, who was experienced as the symbol of the life-awakening sun, indeed as the symbol of the life beyond the grave itself. This is what the pylon would then be proclaiming, "Behold the grave— but know that behind the grave the sun is rising!"

Plate 12. Head of the Sphinx of Giza. Carved from the rock outcrop of a limestone quarry from which King Cheops took the stones for his pyramid. Usually assigned to the reign of Khephren, but possibly older.

III

THE DEATH OF OSIRIS

The History of Egyptian Art

We have seen that the experience of entering the body, and thus the grave, was the single factor which, more than any other, determined the intrinsic nature of Egyptian art. As this art unfolded in the course of its history it brought this aspect of itself to visible expression in work after work. But the rhythmic pattern of the way it did so has a pictorial quality about it that is no less monumental than the works themselves.

Of course, this only becomes evident when instead of the customary classification of Egyptian civilization into "Early Kingdom, Middle Kingdom and New Kingdom" we use a cosmic classification which is more in accordance with Egypt's true nature. A glance at Egyptian history confirms what was being referred to in the previous chapter by the statement that Egypt is a cosmic event. Egyptian history is a kind of record that the stars themselves have left upon the earth.

The present chapter will deal with the rhythmic occurrence of these events. Egyptian culture itself pointed to the existence of such a rhythm with one of its own great mythological pictures.

The Bird Bennu

The Egyptian year had three seasons, which received their rhythm through the regularly recurring flooding of the Nile that fertilized the soil: the flooding season, the sowing season and the season of harvest. However, this "natural year" kept shifting with regard to the "numbered year" because it was calculated with 365 instead of 365¼ days. The beginning of the year, which the Egyptians celebrated at the appearance of Sirius (or Sothis, as they called it), thus gradually moved from one end of the year to the other. Every four years it had shifted a whole day farther and was not "right" again until a certain period of time had elapsed. This was called a *Sothis period* and lasted 365 × 4 or 1,460 years.

This is not the place to go into the deeper justification of the way the Egyptians numbered their years. But we can say that these Sothis periods, which in the final analysis were determined by the universe itself, represent a rhythm that was more than external. They point as well, and mainly, to that great rhythm according to which the whole spiritual development of Egypt ran its course. We will be concerned primarily with the periods from 4242 to 2782, 2782 to 1322 and from 1322 on. These dates, which designate the transition from one Sothis period to the next, are the ones that indicate the real turning points in Egypt's artistic development. The Sothis periods themselves can actually be arrived at by studying the history of Egyptian art. But the opposite is also true; the use of the Sothis periods to date the history of Egyptian art gives it a structure that is both meaningful and natural, whereas no "picture" at all arises if one dates it by "kingdoms."

What this means is that at the transition from one Sothis period to another we find the transition from one definite stage of consciousness to another. For art history is simply recording in the physical the development that man is undergoing in the spiritual. As one epoch changes into the next—and we will be speaking about this more in what follows—consciousness undergoes two processes simultaneously: shrinking, dimming down and submerging, on the one hand, and on the other waking up more and more into new realms of existence.

The Egyptian expressed this in his own way by using a picture.

One of the marvelous symbols which Egypt created and which has never again completely disappeared from human consciousness is that of *the bird Bennu*. We know it by the name the Greeks gave it: the phoenix. Everyone knows the story of how it flies into the fire of the sun, burns up and rises to the sky again out of its own ashes.

It has been claimed that this is a beautiful, but primitive, symbol of the daily death and rebirth of the sun itself. But this interpretation contradicts the fact that the Egyptian never connected this image with such an everyday occurrence. This bird was called the "Lord of Jubilees," and

45

some said that it would only show itself once every 500 years. Other figures that were apparently based on older and more exact knowledge gave the time as once every 1,460 years, the same rhythm as the Sothis period.

The phoenix symbolized the ancient mystery of death and rebirth, and Egypt connected this symbol with the experience of the different epochs of its own development. In doing so it touched upon one of the deepest and most intimate secrets of the universe. The mystery of death and resurrection permeates all living things as the law of their metamorphosis. The Egyptian also felt that his own history was determined by it. But he connected even more with it.

He said that the soul of the sun-god Re rests on the bird Bennu, just as the soul of the creator-god Ptah rests on the Apis bull. The phoenix manifests the innermost essence of the sun. The mystery of death and resurrection is therefore a sun-mystery; in fact, it is *the* sun-mystery. The Egyptian experienced a sun-mystery in the rhythm of his own historical development. We will now have to say something about what this mystery contained.

The Beginnings

The beginnings of Egypt are shrouded in deep darkness. We say this because today we feel that we can only call something "bright" when we have understood it with our modern intellectual consciousness. In Egypt the feeling for such things was just the opposite. When the Egyptians said that in primeval times the gods had ruled over their people like kings, this meant that in those primeval times a spiritual light had been poured out over the land and the people. Such an age has left no essential physical traces of itself, of course, but effects of it are nevertheless clearly evident. For when Egypt finally emerges out of this prehistoric age of light onto the stage of history it is already a "finished product." It does not have to struggle to develop a language of its own; it "speaks Egyptian" right away. The characteristic features of its own unique style are already fully developed, and we see them all in the very first records we have of Egypt's desire to express itself in earthly forms.

This fact has always been a puzzle to historians. It was felt quite rightly that the oldest "pre-dynastic" works of art, such as the Palette of Narmer or the stele of the "Serpent King," are not beginnings at all but results, final achievements of a process of development. The problem is that there are no physical remains that would allow us to trace such a development back. People have tried to regard certain findings that are even older as evidence for one, but these findings are stone-age drawings and sculptures of the sort that have been found scattered all over the earth. They are the remains of a culture that is difficult to date but may be many thousands of years old.

On the one hand, then, we have to assume a long period of what could be called "prenatal" development in Egypt that took place without actually appearing on the level of physical manifestation. At the same time we have to ask what caused the sudden "birth" of this flow of development around the year 3000 B.C., when it incarnated and began to shape the earth in such a characteristic way.

The tremendous dynamism of those first centuries of the development of Egyptian civilization stands out most vividly when we follow the evolution of its architecture from its beginning stages to their culmination in the form of the *pyramid*.

In the previous chapter we pointed out that the seed of all Egyptian architecture is characteristically the grave or "mastaba." The sides of this flat, rectangular brick structure slope gently toward the center. The mastaba itself is found either over a walled-up pit that reaches deep down into the earth or over a chamber hollowed out of a rock. The greater part of the structure is thus hidden inside the earth. The whole thing is one single mass, except for the chamber into which the corpse was lowered, a separate room for the dead person's statue and another small chamber for offerings. This form was established early on and was preserved for several centuries until a new development set in shortly after the year 3000, when changes began to take place at a very rapid rate.

Djoser, the pharaoh who founded the 3rd Dynasty and began to rule around the year 2980,* first had a large brick mastaba built for himself in the traditional form. Later on, however, he had a new structure built—as though the first one had not been a fully satisfactory expression for what

*For dates see the section on "The Problem of Chronology" in the Supplement.

he had in mind. *Imhotep* has traditionally been regarded as its actual creator. The man behind this name seems to have been one of Egypt's foremost initiates. He has been remembered for thousands of years, not only as one of the great master builders, but as an outstanding priest and healer who could perform miracles as well. His *Step Pyramid of Sakkara* was, first of all, nothing but a stack of six mastabas that remained unchanged as to both their form and their rectangular ground plan. At the same time, the pyramid attained the respectable height of 58 meters and was the first decisive step toward a major new development (Plate 13; Fig. 5).

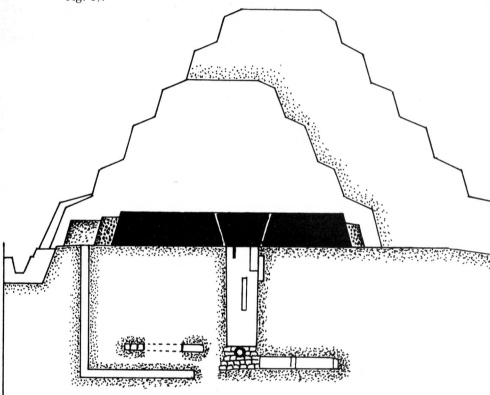

Fig. 5. Sakkara. Cross-section through the Step Pyramid from east to west. Black area: the original mastaba. The 28 m shaft extending down from it leads to the king's coffin chamber made of granite and to the adjoining rooms filled with household utensils and partially lined with faience. To the left (east), one of the 32 m deep shafts leading to the burial chambers of the queen and the king's children.

Plate 13. Step Pyramid of King Djoser in Sakkara. The 60 m high pyramid stands within a 545 x 278 m sacred area along with several other structures. The whole area is surrounded by a wall 10 m high.

Another noteworthy feature of this step pyramid is the fact that it is no longer made of bricks but of cut stone. In fact, the Egyptians regarded Imhotep himself as the inventor of the art of stonecutting.

The next step in the course of this development is the Pyramid of *Snefru*, the pharaoh who founded the 4th Dynasty and began to reign around 2930. It is known as the *Pyramid of Medum* after the place near which he had it built. It is also a step pyramid, but this time the ground plan is square and the individual steps are placed one on top of the other in such a way that their upper edges lie along a single straight line. In this way the pure pyramid made its first appearance in the form of an idea. The only thing left to do was to express it in material form by filling in the open spaces. This was then done when the so-called *Red Pyramid* was built near Dahshur. It is still ascribed to the same pharaoh and is already nearly 100 meters high.

The culmination of this development is the *Pyramid of Cheops*, built by Snefru's successor and named for him. It is roughly 147 meters high, about twice the height of a really tall church tower, and the length of each edge at the base is about 230 meters.

It is hard to imagine just how massive this structure is. Calculations have shown that it contains approximately 2,300,000 stone blocks weighing an average of 2½ tons each. In order to understand what demands this building made on human labor—in other words, on the human will—we must also take into consideration that the material for it had to be quarried 15 kilometers away, on the other side of the Nile. The limestone for the casing came from even farther away, and the different granites for the king's chamber and the anteroom were brought all the way from the region of Aswan, a distance of nearly 1000 kilometers. Some of these granite blocks are 7 meters long and weigh 16-20 tons each. Modern engineers are at a loss to explain how the workers managed to solve the tremendous problems of transporting and working all this stone with the undoubtedly very simple technology available in those days, especially since, once on the site, the stones had to be raised to heights of considerably more than 100 meters. The only solution is to assume that the people of that time had a physical strength at their disposal that was quite different from ours today because of the way it may have been connected with a type of consciousness that was also still quite different.

The *Pyramid of Khephren* (2875-?), who was supposedly the second of Cheops' successors, is almost as large as the Pyramid of Cheops, with a height of 143 meters and a base edge length of 215 meters. But with it the force for such a mighty impulse seems exhausted. (Plate 14). The pyramid that Khephren's successor *Mycerinus* built next to the two mighty structures of his predecessors is only half their height, and after this both size and quality of workmanship in any new buildings greatly diminish.

The picture we obtain from contemplating this century-long architectural development makes a very strong impression. We see a structure,

Plate 14. The Great Pyramids of Giza. From the right, the pyramids of Cheops, Khephren and Mycerinus. The apex of the Pyramid of Khephren still has a small part of the original covering of polished limestone.

the major and most esential part of which has been resting under the ground for hundreds of years, emerge from its womb and grow to a gigantic height. A tremendous impulse must have set to work here, and we can at least guess at the nature of its source.

The century in which this process took place was of the highest significance for Egyptian culture. The year 2907, almost the very year in which this development culminated, marked an important cosmic event, the transition of the spring equinox of the sun into the constellation of Taurus. This signalled the *beginning of the Egyptian cultural epoch*, which was under the sign of the bull. What we can follow step by step in this mighty growth of a grave out of the womb of the earth is the earthly counterpart and utmost physical manifestation of a tremendous spiritual birth process. Out of its former obscurity the genius of Egypt emerged here full of power.

Today such a statement will probably be understood to mean that people of those times had decided to represent such things intentionally. This, of course, is not what we mean at all. Men and the souls of men were only the gateways through which superhuman powers did their work. We have no idea what these people experienced in their souls. We can only suppose that since they were more receptive and "transparent" than we are today, they were well aware of how a tremendous process of birth was taking place within the whole organism of the cosmos. Certain stories that they told do, in fact, point to a very clear awareness on their part of the dying away of an old world-age and the birth of a new one. Later on we will have to examine another one of these tales. But if they did have an awareness of these things, it was of such a nature that, with it, they attended to a process that was taking place objectively, with no participation on their part, and they tried to follow this process devotedly with their whole being, including their hands, their will and their whole body. This is how the pyramids came to be.

This becomes quite clear when we try to characterize the essential nature of these structures on the basis of their form. What each one expressed as a work of art is less important for our present purpose than what its cultic function was. For what appearance did it present? Nothing less than that of a gigantic crystal, encased in its cloak of polished limestone slabs and glistening almost painfully in the sun. The king's funerary chamber, however—that room for the sake of which the whole superhuman effort had been made—lay deeply hidden inside it and was completely inaccessible. The two or three other rooms were hidden also, as were the corridors that led to them. In fact, no one could even guess which of the external slabs that fitted together so perfectly the entrance corridor was under. Once the pyramid was finished and the king who had built it had been buried, no one was ever to set foot in it again.

In spite of all this, the building was an infinitely artistic organism. There were exact mathematical relationships between the length, breadth and height of the individual rooms, their position within the pyramid, the angle of inclination of the corridors, and the various measurements of length, breadth, height and angles of the pyramid as a whole. (Once again special reference is made to the above-mentioned book by E. Bindel, *Die ägyptischen Pyramiden als Zeugen vergangener Mysterienweisheit*, reprinted 1975.) These buildings were a mathematical experience. Ultimately this has to do with the crystalline character of their being as a whole. They must have seemed to be full of light. The angle of their sides was such that for the greater part of the day they not only did not cast any shadows but also had no shadows on any of their sides. They must have looked like shadowless, purest light—a "poetic condensation" of the forces of light itself.

Such a "mathematical experience," however, meant much more to the people of those times than what we connect with this concept today.

Egyptian mathematics had already developed to a remarkably high degree. Even so, the Egyptian could not carry out certain mathematical functions which we find very simple. For example, he was unable to divide. Whenever he needed to do this, he had to go through some very complicated steps of finding out how many times it was possible to multiply. Egyptian mathematics was of a completely different *sort* than ours. It was not yet abstract and intellectual but more intuitive. And it was still intimately interwoven with other disciplines, especially music.

Today we know in an abstract way that musical relationships are based on numerical relationships. The Egyptian must still have been able to experience this directly. The "Quadrivium," which consisted of Arithmetic, Geometry, Music and Astronomy—in contrast to the "Trivium" of Logic, Physics and Metaphysics—originated in antiquity and designated a specific stage of higher learning well on into the Middle Ages. In Egypt it must still have been experienced as a unity: *numerical* relationships, as *geometric* pictures in which *cosmic* relationships became visible, wove themselves together into *musical* experiences.

53

There are echoes of such experiences down into comparatively recent times. At the beginning of the modern age (1480 A.D.) Tinctoris, in his "Diffinitorium musicae," distinguished three kinds of musical experience: 1. Cosmic music, the great rhythms and movements of the cosmos, of which the circling orbits of the stars are only the "visible" part. 2. Human music, the music of the microcosm, the human body. This music becomes "visible" in the rhythms of life. 3. Man-made music—the only kind we consider to be music today, but which Tinctoris could still regard merely as attempts to reveal the other, "higher" music to the world (Fig. 6).

Two hundred fifty years later Leibniz wrote in a letter: "Music is a hidden arithmetical exercise of the soul, which does not know that in experiencing music it is working with numbers . . ." He was still faintly aware of the secret, but by now it was "hidden."

Perhaps it will now be clear what we mean when we say that for the

Fig. 6. Reconstruction of the pyramid area of Giza. At the bank of the Nile stands the entrance building, from which a covered corridor leads to the temple of the dead at the pyramid. Around the Pyramid of Cheops (to the right) are smaller pyramids and mastabas, tombs of relatives of the pharaoh and various dignitaries.

Egyptian the pyramids must have been something he could hear. He must have taken them in, not only with his head but with his whole body, in terms of all their relationships, and then had a musical experience of them which included an experience of cosmic powers and relationships as well.

The same must be said of the other architectural documents of that time which have been preserved well enough for us to be able to reconstruct their external appearance. These are the *temples of the dead* situated in front of the pyramids. They were arranged in such a way that whoever came to the festivities was received by a large entrance building on the bank of the river. On the right and the left was an entrance, each flanked by two sphinxes. Through one of these the person entering would go into a corridor which immediately turned at a right angle and led him into an anteroom to meet whoever might have come in through the other entrance. From here he could go through another corridor into the great hall of pillars, a large space constructed in wonderful proportions which actually consisted of two spaces fitted together at right angles to each other. Georg Steindorff writes about this in his book, *Die Kunst der Ägypter* (*The Art of the Egyptians*, Leipzig, 1928): ". . . a massive block of masonry, in which the rooms have been hollowed out as if in a rock. Its main room is of the utmost simplicity: a hall in the form of an inverted T with smooth, plain walls; a flat ceiling supported by sixteen monolithic granite pillars; in front of these, statues of the king, larger than life, were seated on thrones in grave solemnity. There is probably no other Egyptian monumental building in which sculpture has been so successfully placed at the service of architecture as it has been in this hall. In addition, one must speak of the wonderful harmony of the colors: the dazzling white of the alabaster floor, the shining red of the granite surfaces and the greenish stone of the statues. The whole is of the most rigorous objectivity, a model of *applied geometry* . . ."

The actual temple of the dead at the foot of the pyramid, which is reached through a covered corridor almost 500 meters long, can be described in much the same way. In fact, it would probably be more appropriate to describe it as "music frozen in stone" than as "applied geometry." The sublime grandeur of this structure can already be sensed from its floor plan. The two "tones" of the "Broad Hall" and the "Deep Hall," resounding together as wonderfully organized spaces in themselves, and the open "Court of Statues," which was widened out even more by the open-

55

ings that led from it into the ambulatory which completely surrounded it, must have resulted in a marvelous harmony of spatial relationships. For besides these elements nothing else was present: no pictures, no inscriptions, nothing but plain walls (Fig. 7).

All these elements together constitute a *tomb*, erected over the deceased pharaoh who has now become Osiris, a shining god. "The gods who used to be are now resting in their pyramids," according to an old song from the 11th Dynasty. One was really aware that the dead man was still living there in his wonderful, gleaming house, that he was actually present there and would remain so for all eternity. But in the texts that have been found on sarcophagi or on the walls of later pyramids he says about his life and his pathway after death: "The god (i.e., the dead pharaoh) is coming in peace! say the inhabitants of the great moon. May they, along with Re, give me their radiance . . ."

Or: ". . . Heaven is raging, the stars are quaking, the zodiac sign of the Archer is trembling and the 'bones of the Akeru demons' are growing unsteady; for they have noticed a striding and have seen the Pharaoh and how he appeared and his soul was like that of a god . . ."

And then the strange observation: "I find Orion standing on the road with his scepter in his hand. I raise the scepter and take hold of it, that in so doing I may become divine. He gives me the scepter which is in his hand and says: 'Come to me, my son! The rising (of the star) takes place in peace. May your mummy be near my place; you are my son, the master of my house.'"

The dead pharaoh, resting in his pyramid "in peace" and ceremoniously embalmed, is wandering among the stars of heaven. But this is only a contradiction for someone who makes the kind of abstract separation between heaven and earth that we are compelled to make today. The resolution of this paradox can hardly be better expressed than with the words R. M. Rilke used at the close of one of his "Stories of God":

". . .'Is God *there* then?' he asked. I said nothing. Then I bent down to him and said, 'Ewald, are we really *here*?' ."

Who is to say that for the Egyptian the stars were "up there" and we "down here"? It was the secret of that first period of Egypt that the stars were not yet "there"—because human beings were not yet "here."

That is the tremendous experience of the pyramids and of the architecture connected with them in that first period. In the previous chapter we described how this fact lived in the sculpture of that age when we

56

Fig. 7. Ground plan of Khephren's entrance building and temple of the dead. The terrace (1) of the temple in the valley was reached by ascending to it from the bank of the branch of the Nile. The path between two pairs of sphinxes, through narrow corridors and into the mighty block of stone then led first into an ante-room (2) and from there into the Hall of Pillars (3), whose ceiling was supported by mighty granite pillars 4.2 m high. 23 statues of the pharaoh stood along the walls. From the Hall of Pillars a covered corridor (4) 494 m in length led to the temple of the dead built against the wall that surrounded the pyramid. From there the way again led through an ante-room (5) into a "Broad" Hall (6) and then into a "Deep" Hall (7). All these spaces must be imagined as immersed in a dim light coming in through narrow openings. Finally, the path led out into bright daylight again in the "Court of Statues" (8). The "public" temple seems to have ended here, where the sacrificial altar stood under the watchful gaze of 12 statues of either the pharaoh or of other gods. The five statues of the pharaoh that represented his various names and were located inside the statue chambers (9) had a part in these sacrifices as well. It is hard to imagine what a wealth of ritualistic activity must have unfolded along this whole path. Beyond this point, more corridors built at right angles to each other led into rooms where the daily "service" was performed in the sanctuary (10), most likely by the priests alone.

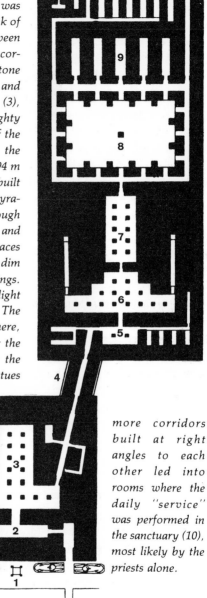

discussed the diorite statue of Chephren with the Sun-falcon behind his head. It is the experience of the grave. But the grave becomes the place where heaven is present, where the harmony of the spheres resounds, where the stars are singing and "Re" is uttering his WORD.

"Mathematics is the life of the gods." (Novalis)

It has already been pointed out that Egyptian culture in the age of the pyramids is not a primitive beginning but the result of a development that had taken place during a preceding period. In its last few hundred years, this period had begun to take hold of the earth and inscribe into it something that it had to say, having heard the call of the angel of a new age of human history.

We know very little about this period, but strangely enough, we do know of an important event that marks its beginning. In the year 4241, a calendar was introduced in the area around Memphis that remained in use throughout the entire Egyptian age. This event coincides with the beginning of a Sothis period in 4242. Because of it, we know that there must have been a highly developed culture in Egypt at that time, and this fact points us back to an even earlier period. Later on, this Egyptian calendar was introduced into Rome by Julius Caesar as the best one then available, and it was then used in Europe until the Middle Ages. The fact that in spite of this we know so little about this period actually tells us something about its nature. For if it had not yet really taken hold of the earth, this means that it had also not yet really come down to the earth with its consciousness. "The gods were ruling the land." But one could just as well say that human beings were still living among the gods. What confronts us in the age of the pyramids is only a last fading away of this consciousness. But even this is so overwhelming that today we can still only grope for words in our stammering efforts to express what it was actually like.

This experience of fading away and of the dawning of something new at the same time is expressed in a story connected with the name of the greatest of the pyramid builders. As the story goes, "Cheops and his sons had once been discussing the miracles of the great wise men of old. When one of the young princes then remarked that a magician who could perform such miracles was still alive, the king sent him out to find the wise man and bring him back. After the man had shown them a few examples of his miraculous arts, he reluctantly agreed to answer a question the king had asked: The wife of a priest of Re, he said, would soon give birth to three children whom Re himself would have conceived, and all three would become kings and rule over Egypt. When he saw that this news had saddened the king, he assured him that there was no need to worry and went on to say, 'Your son, his son, and only then one of them,' meaning, 'Your son shall rule, then your grandson and after him one of these three children.' . . . The names that these children received from the three disguised gods who were present at their birth are Userkaf, Sahure and Kakai, the names of the first three kings of the 5th Dynasty" (J. H. Breasted, *History of Egypt*, Berlin, 1910).

This tale is not only a pious fraud on the part of the priests of Re, whose intention it was to glorify "their" dynasty at the expense of the previous one, but also an extremely impressive record of the significance of this transition itself.

We will have more to say about it later, for the transition from the 4th to the 5th dynasty also marks the end of one Sothis period and the beginning of a new one.[8]

The Sons of Re

During the 5th Dynasty, the art of pyramid building declines more and more. The pyramid is no longer regarded as the "royal" tomb, meant for the king alone. People of rank and wealth now appropriate it for their own use as well. In the early days the core consisted of carefully cut stone blocks; more and more this gives way to one made of air-dried bricks or quarry-stone, while only the outer casing is still made of limestone slabs carefully fitted together. From now on all energy and reverence are devoted to a new form of sanctuary: the great *sun temples of the 5th Dynasty* that begin to spring up (about 2750-2625).

If we compare their form with one of the great pyramid complexes, we see immediately that this is what they grew out of. The same elements recur: an entrance building on the river bank, a covered corridor leading up to the level of the plateau, and a temple at the edge of an enclosing wall. Even the obelisk which now stands in the center of the sacred area in place of the pyramid cannot hide the fact that the pyramid was the origin of its form. The Greeks still even called its peak the "pyramidion."

The form of these sanctuaries grew out of that older form. But the difference between the earlier form and the later one is crucial: the force that determines the latter's shape is no longer a god descending to the earth from the starry heavens but rather a force growing upward out of the earth that raises the pyramidion up into the air. The growth of the pyramid from above downwards was infinitely sublime, outwards from its non-spatial peak into the broad quadrangle of its base, raying down from above and spreading out more and more. The obelisk stretches up. But the sun temples are not yet those slender arrows that shoot upwards so sharply later on. There is still the heaviness in them of an immense mass raising itself up step by step because the "weight" of everything it carries along with it from afar is so enormous. In these temples, the very immensity of this process—the weight of the world itself—has found a form (Fig. 8).

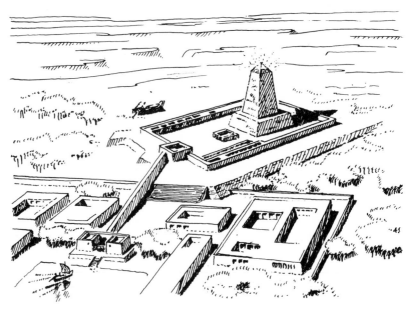

Fig. 8. Reconstruction of a sun temple from the 5th dynasty. In the foreground, the entrance temple at the bank of the Nile. At the left, behind the sanctuary, the cultic boat of the sun god, made of bricks. Because the pyramidion, or apex of the obelisk, was gilded, the rising sun could be seen shining down from it even while it was actually still hidden below the horizon. One wonders . . . could this have been the origin of the saying about the "sunrise from on high"?

The pyramid is dying and the obelisk is being born. We must try to feel in the grandeur of this event that it is one of the points of history which, for the Egyptian, was surrounded by the mystery of the Bird Bennu. One world is dying away and a new one is coming into being.

The architecture of this period makes it surprisingly clear what sphere man is now awakening into.

The architecture of the entire first period of Egyptian culture was dominated by the *pillar*. Gigantic monoliths, smoothly cut and polished, lent a wonderful solemnity and a stern objectivity to the rooms and spaces which they organized and widened. Their stern beauty lay in the harmony of the measurements they brought into these rooms and in the harmonious organization of the rooms themselves.

Now, however, in the temples of the 5th Dynasty the *column* suddenly appears. Imhotep has, of course, already employed three-quarter columns here and there in his temple buildings. But on the one hand these are not free-standing, freely growing forms yet; on the other, in terms of their structure as a whole, they are nothing but "round (or rather: half-round) pillars." The freely growing column with its capital of living plants only comes to be invented now because before this time it has never really been an inner experience. For the world of life-forces out of which these columns grew (see the remarks on this topic in Chapter 2) is the one into which man is just now waking up. From the world of the stars he is coming down into the regions of the earth. But in this period he does not quite touch the realm of the physical yet, the world of what has "become." He has first to remain in the in-between world of the etheric, where things are still "becoming" and taking shape.

The fact that from now on the temple walls begin to be covered with *wall paintings* and *reliefs* on a large scale is connected with this. Where sounds were heard in earlier times there is now a boundless abundance of pictures. We are still able to experience the latter part of this process, at least, in an abbreviated form. This happens when from the starry depths of night we return to the "house" of our body, passing through the sphere of living formative forces where the images of our dreams are born. If we keep this in mind, we can understand both the emergence and the inherent character of Egyptian painting and relief work in a deeper sense. We must now take at least a brief look at these.

Egyptian drawing does not use perspective yet. It remains entirely within the two-dimensional surface. Figures are drawn larger or smaller, not because they are supposed to appear closer or farther away, but because their relative size indicates whether they are more or less important in an inner sense. Gods are large and human beings are small; kings are large while their servants and subjects are small.

The principle of foreshortening is also unknown. In its place, a "law of frontality" leads to that strange kind of drawing in which the head and lower extremities appear in profile but the body itself, or at least the upper part of it, is viewed directly from the front.

What this means is that in the final analysis the pictorial art of Egypt has no concept of the "illusory" world of space as yet. This is certainly not because this art was too primitive or because the people themselves were not sufficiently gifted—who would ever say that?—but because this whole world of images was experienced in a sphere which is still outside of, or "before," the world of physical space. Its reality is an inner one and has nothing in common with the world of "external appearances" at all.

Now these walls are not only covered with pictures but with writing as well. That strange *writing passion* of the Egyptian begins, a passion that very soon stops at nothing any more and ends by covering the walls, columns, doors and finally even statues with sacred texts. There are statues from a later period that have hieroglyphs all over them except for their heads. The Egyptian seems to be possessed by something. What is going on here?

The Egyptian did not experience writing yet as a mere process of communicating some information or other by means of abstract symbols. For him it was an activity that went far beyond anything else that a human being could do. The scribe ranked himself much higher than he did the artists (and *what* artists they were, indeed!). We can understand what feelings filled the Egyptian as he wrote by looking at, say, the "Statue of a Scribe" in the Louvre in Paris. There he sits, painting the sacred characters onto the papyrus leaf that lies outstretched on his crossed legs and gazing into an infinite distance with a heavenly glow on his face. As they write, they look into a wonderful, glowing distance, for writing is almost an act of speaking, an activity that involves the "Word." It is not a speaking that can actually be heard, of course, but one that only comes about in the movements of the runic signs themselves.

God is beginning to grow silent, but he still communicates through signs. HIS breath wafts through that world of images which was the substance of Egyptian picture-writing. In a higher sphere the working of Re, the activity of the Logos, is still perceived as the mighty, creative WORD that moves the world. Here in this sphere it reveals itself as the weaving, formative life-force that also creates pictures. The world is no longer a chorale sung by the stars, but it *is* still a holy book both filled with and continually adding to its collection of wonderful runes. The Egyptian must still have felt something like a never-ending writing movement in the entire living world around him. It was movement that affected the true "scribe" so deeply that he actually seemed to be possessed by it.

This is why the art of writing was so very sacred and constituted a high priesthood in itself. Man, as he writes, is the revelation of the working of the Logos in the creative sphere of the formative forces.

But now we must look once more at the sun temples and finally at the story with which the previous chapter closed.

The obelisks were symbols of the sun. The fact that the peak of the obelisk was gilded is at least a hint of what kind of celebrations took place at the large altar in front of the obelisk. From the first rays of the rising sun there must have been a mysterious glow around it in the early morning hours while the rest of the world, including the walled court-yard in which the worshippers had gathered, was still shrouded in dim, nocturnal twilight. Up on the peak, however, the god was already mys-teriously present. This is why one of these temples was called "Re's favorite place." We see from this that it was not really the physical sun that was the object of reverence (for it was still below the horizon), but rather the power of its rising. This is what the people experienced as it came down to them from the peak of the obelisk, and they took it in deeply.

Now we can see more clearly what the significance of these obelisks actually is. We have already spoken of their force of erectness. The fact that they are built at all is a sign that man is beginning to experience this force of erectness as an essential part of his own nature. But the force of the obelisk is the power of the rising sun. The power to stand upright is this sun-power internalized. What radiates down from the sun into the rest of the living world from outside it, so that the plants lift their stalks and blossoms upwards, has now entered into man as a force which is peculiarly his own. What fills him as his sense of egohood when he straightens up is originally the feeling of his own sun-like nature. It is the power of the "dawning from on high," as it will be called much later (Luke 1:78) on the basis of similar experiences, when all these temples will long since have passed away. Such experiences, however, will then be taking place in a purely spiritual realm.

This is also the deeper meaning of the tale of King Cheops about how the kings of the next dynasty will be "Sons of Re." They will share in his substance, which will be a part of their own. The priestess, "Soul of Man," will give birth to "the Son" out of the power of the sun. This is how the mysteries expressed the fact that man was now beginning to "find himself upon the earth," even if at first he was only in that region at the very boundary of the physical, earthly element.

This development was very soon complete. Shortly afterwards, presumably during the 6th Dynasty, the Egyptian temples as we know them came into being. After this, their basic form, with its gigantic pylon, the doorways, the wall that has to be broken through and all the experiences of awakening and coming to oneself, as these were depicted in the previous chapter, remained unchanged for thousands of years. The "Sons of Re" were born.

The Sons of the Widow

The sons of Re now reign for over a thousand years. But the "ego" that has been born is only an illusory one at first. It bears within it the consequences of man's rebellion against the gods and of his exodus from the silence of obedience. It bears the germ of death, and death will grow — to monstrous proportions.

The Sothis period just depicted in its beginning stages lasts until 1322. About 200 years before this, however, there are already signs that this period is on the wane and that something new is stirring. One can feel the beating of the Bird Bennu's wings again.

On all sides we now notice a strange architectural urge to move directly into the rock, into the bones of the earth. King *Amenophis/ Amenhotep I* (about 1550) is the first to abandon the customary practice of burying the pharaoh in a pyramid by having a *rock tomb* built for himself. His successor, *Thutmose I*, then builds the first of a long series of rock tombs in the Valley of the Kings. This break with tradition was by no means a thoughtless undertaking. People have tried to explain it by saying that places were sought where the corpse, which had been carefully and ceremoniously embalmed, would be safer from grave robbers than in a pyramid. Such considerations may have played a role in the final decision, but the question then arises as to why no one had thought of doing this sooner. It is surely much more important that the possibility of abandoning the pyramid was entertained at all, or that one could even consider that the dead king would feel better in a room carved into the rock.

What is actually happening is that people are becoming inwardly acquainted with the hard, rigid, dead rock-bones of the earth. The proof of this is that shortly afterwards the temple itself begins to be built into the natural rock. There was certainly no external practical reason for this. About 1480 Queen *Hatshepsut* had a mighty temple built in Deir-el-Bahri, the inner rooms of which were already driven into the natural rock.[9] A little over 150 years later, in exactly 1322, the pharaoh *Haremhab* (1350-1315) built the *Cliff Temple of Geb-el-Adde*, which was not built entirely inside the rock. The most powerful evidence of this will to enter the bony structure of the earth is probably the cliff temple that *Ramesses II* (about 1250) built, or rather, had carved out of the mountain in *Abu Simbel*. The ceiling of one of its halls is supported by statues over 10 meters high, and it is 55 meters from the threshold to the far end of the rooms. Today we can hardly imagine what it must have meant to drive those enormous spaces deep into the rock and to carve such collossal statues out of natural rock for the facade. A gigantic will to achieve something almost impossible must have been at work behind it (Plate 15).

Until now the temple has been an impressive expression of the silence of the grave, closed off and sternly drawing people into the fearful, narrow limits of its earthly space. Suddenly this is no longer enough. The all-permeating light and the wind, wafting from far away, are now not even allowed to play around the outer walls. No longer may the stars look down on it, nor the bright eye of the sun. This is the home of the god: the place where the earth has died and become the powerful, elemental expression of absolute silence.

This period is also noted for two events of external history, at least one of which had a visible effect on Egypt's artistic development. This is the reign of *Amenophis IV (Akhenaton)* (1375-1357?) and the spiritual revolution which he introduced (even though it only lasted until his death).

Plate 15. Cliff Temple of Abu Simbel. Entrance to the larger of the two temples which were carved directly into the rock wall rising out of the Nile. On both sides are 20 m high statues of Ramesses II (19th dynasty, 1290-1223 B.C.). The small, nearly lifesize figures at his feet are sons and daughters, his mother and his wife. In the niche above the entrance is the falconheaded Horus with the King's name. The temple goes back 50 m into the rock.

In him a man came to the throne of an enormous empire at the height of its power who was nothing but a human being. That was his tragedy. Even if his magnificent "Hymn to the Sun" had not been preserved; even if we did not know that he was trying to found a religion that honestly recognized the silence of the ancient gods and sought to span whatever part of heaven could still be reached; even if we could not tell from all this that he was the first person to act out of a consciousness restricted almost entirely to what can be attained in a purely physical, human way, we could still know all this from the art works that he sponsored: the art of Tell el-Amarna. Countless copies of some of these works are to be found all over the world.

What speaks to us in such a gripping way when we look at them is their very humanness. The works of earlier centuries, even the stone portraits themselves, never look out at us as human beings. They are gods or, at the very least, beings who have no other function than to serve as unquestioning vessels for the commands of some super-human, super-personal agency. They are scribes who follow this one calling with their whole being; they are pharaohs, priests or princesses—and nothing else.

Suddenly we have real people. King and queen, mother and child, officials, priests, physicians—whoever they may be, we find ourselves deeply moved by the personal destinies and experiences that we sense in connection with what they have to do in life. Their human souls suffer and are happy, feel the melancholy of the world, tremble at the magnitude of an infinite task and are blessed by the presence of other human beings. These are real people!

It is one thing to let ourselves be carried away by this pure and infinitely tender beauty; it is quite another to see that at last man is beginning to speak for himself because, once and for all, the gods have fallen silent.

This is why relief-pictures now appear that depict with an almost touching delicacy the life of a pharaoh who dares to be a human being: "The King with his Family," "The King with his Wife," "The King at his Palace Window." And we must also understand that the priests, who were the guardians of the tradition, were so terror-stricken at the actions of this "heretic" that immediately after his death they chiseled his name off every stone on which it had been inscribed, as if it were something devilish, and leveled the new capital that he had built at Tell el-Amarna to the ground. A pharaoh who does not completely lose himself in service to his higher calling destroys the foundations of pharaoh-hood, the god-willed principles that support the kingdom itself. The striving of the priests of the old gods for power was not the only thing that made them act the way they did, even though at this time decadent magic begins to find its way into the Egyptian mysteries. There is tragedy in the destiny of this king, the tragedy of a man born too soon.

This may well also be the delicate veil that lies over all the works that portray Akhenaton and Nefertiti. We feel they would like to tear this veil apart, but are powerless to even make a hole in it. The life in their faces and in their limbs presses against it and yet remains spellbound like a bud trying to bloom before its time.

The truth is that at this time Egypt is shaking in its very foundations. What has happened?

The architecture of this period tells us. We only need to look and read what it records, namely, that this is the time when man enters a new realm or world-space: the kingdom of the physical, the really solid mineral region of the earth. Descended first from the resounding worlds of stars, he has passed through the sphere of plantlike life; now he strikes against the rock of the earth itself. This is the time when he fully awakens to find himself, his existence as a human being, his personal destiny and his freedom. But it is also the sphere of silence, in which things are no longer becoming but have already become.

Egypt's development now comes to an end. Its architecture is the result of a long, slow upward climb of the grave. In ancient times the mastaba had slumbered deep in the bowels of the earth. Then it grew upwards to become the pyramid, the obelisk and the pylon of the temple. Now, in the cliff temples, the earth itself becomes the pylon, in other words, the mastaba or grave. It becomes the grave of the cosmos, and all the creative power of the cosmos itself dies into it. For death itself is growing.

Isis, the infinite, mysterious Mother of Worlds, has become a widow. That wonderful myth, which has resounded through the whole of Egyptian culture from its earliest beginnings onward, now becomes reality. Osiris, the divine, sunlike Word of Worlds, who is also her brother and spouse, has been placed in the coffin and finally cut to pieces and scattered about. (Set, the Dark One, has done this; he who had an ass's head and was therefore the image of the one animal that is more at home in in what is rigid and earthly than any other.) Whoever was initiated as far as the sphere of the great Mother of Worlds was deeply shocked to experience her there as both a widow and barren. The initiations of the pyramid builders had been quite different. They had still experienced their own death in the initiation itself and their rebirth out of the divine world-womb of Isis, reawakened by the word and the creative power of Osiris. They thus had every right to call themselves "Horus in the Palace." The direct presence of the Divine One, raying down from worlds of light, had been a real experience for them. They *were* Horus, the son of Isis and Osiris. Now, however, the silence of the grave had entered those spheres

68

as well, and man was deeply shaken by the experience of himself there as: the son of the widow, the barren one.

Among the sculptures of this latter period a motif appears that illustrates all this in a shattering way. There are statues of a man squatting on the ground with his knees pulled up and his arms around them. The body is completely covered by his cloak, so that the whole form is little more than a cubical block with a human head looking out the top. Everything else is inside the stone block itself, immersed in a deep and powerful silence. Man has been laid into the grave (Plate 16).

The End

We look up from all this with a question. Is this the end? What was it all for?

The urgency of this question becomes even greater when we consider the following fact: Now that Egypt has really arrived at the goal of its centuries-long journey, it shies away from it and does not *want* to die. The whole final period of Egyptian culture is a desperate attempt to hang on to an element that was still alive in former times. Akhenaton, who in a certain way brought Egypt's path to its logical fulfillment, has simply been wiped out—extinguished. After him, art as well knows nothing but tradition.

Egypt does not want to die, and so its dark magic arises: that desperate clinging to forces of magic at the very time in which it has already witnessed the birth of man as an ego-being, and therefore of egotism itself. The Caesar-cult of the pharaohs comes into being, and its excesses know no bounds. It is the living pharaoh, not the dead one, who is now worshipped as a god. The pharaohs' unlimited striving for power has begun.

Is this the end?

For the answer to this, we must look at the second of the two historical events mentioned earlier which occurred at the time when the previous Sothis-period was dying out and this last one was just beginning. This may have taken place shortly after the events connected with Akhenaton had run their course. At this time the little tribe of Hebrews

went out of the land of Egypt and conquered a new space in which to live. For half a millenium they had been absorbing Egyptian culture and, according to reliable accounts, their leader, Moses, had been initiated into the Egyptian mysteries. It is said that when they left they took with them the Egyptians' gold and silver temple vessels. This does not mean, however, that they stole real objects of such value. It means that they took with them what the forces of the sun mysteries (the golden vessels) and those of the moon-mysteries (the silver vessels) permitted them to absorb and carry.

After 1322 B.C. the history of Egypt really continues on in Palestine, until the time when the WORD found a "vessel" there, walked the earth, was laid in the grave of the earth and transformed that grave into the birthplace of a new world. The mystery of the Bird Bennu, the Mystery of the Sun, is at last fulfilled.

Plate 16. Stone block statue of the priest, Petamenophis. On the front the priest can be seen praying before Osiris. About 600 B.C. Black granite.

IV

THE MESSAGE OF MAN

The Mission of Greece

It will always remain a mystery how humanity could ever blossom into that wondrous dream that we call Greece. For a dream is all it was, a fleeting smile on the face of man on his journey through the ages. The actual glorious golden age of Greece hardly lasted a hundred years—three generations. Its ascent was rapid and urgent; what followed was just as rapid and relentless. The dream was brief, but it had such a fragrance, a glow, a sound about it that men wept when they remembered it again two thousand years later. *Hyperion, Empedocles, Iphigenia*—all these works were songs that praised this dream. Not one of them is without its deep melancholy, and many a verse in them is a single sob.

"Noble simplicity and quiet grandeur" was a phrase coined in the days of Winckelmann, Hölderlin and Goethe. We have long since known that this is not the way things were; that Greece, too, trembled as it felt the dark, terrible, primal forces of existence. What later generations were able to envision through those words and pictures was a far cry from the longing that moved the soul of the Greek, a longing that again and again became a reality—and not only in the material substance of a work of art—the longing for the *truly human.*

This melody begins so softly, as none other ever did; hardly perceptible at first somewhere in the chaos and darkness, it gradually becomes more distinct, rises up at last in *one* great arc, increasing in its radiance—until at last, long after it has passed away, it still sheds a wondrous, gentle glow on whatever is at all receptive. If one despairs already at the prospect of describing Egypt, because our words have lost so much of their former power and their grandeur, how much more must one not despair at the attempt to describe Greece, because they are also no longer permeated as strongly by the breath of beauty and no longer move freely enough under a wide expanse of open sky, graced and ensouled by Father Ether.

Let us begin our reflections again with a picture from mythology. Among the great heroes of antiquity, from whose deeds Greece felt that its own soul had been born, Perseus, one of the sons of Zeus, has a position of special prominence. His great deed was his victory over Medusa, and the influence of this deed down through the ages was guaranteed since Athena herself preserved it.

Medusa is described as a dreadful monster: "Her head was covered with dragon's scales and with snakes instead of hair; she had big tusks like a hog's, brazen hands and golden wings." Whoever looked at her was turned to stone. Perseus approached her as she slept, walking backwards and using his brazen shield as a mirror to catch her reflection. This is how he was finally able to cut off her head. But the moment he did so, who should spring forth from her but Pegasus. Athena then took Medusa's head and attached it to her shield, where it became a fearful weapon.

What does this deed mean?

We can get several clues from a Medusa head called the "sleeping Medusa" that stems from the time of Greece but is kept in Rome. Surprisingly, this being is not a repulsive one at all; on the contrary, her beauty is quite striking. But there are dangerous depths in her relaxed appearance. She is like the night itself. And indeed, that *is* Medusa: the heiress of an ancient, nocturnal, dreamlike consciousness not yet confined to earthly limits. This is why one sees it writhing out of her head like snakes (Plate 17) and why she is experienced as a winged relative of the dragon. But why is she so frightening for man?

This experience is the end result of a development that had already begun in Egypt. The Egyptian had already learned that whoever rebelled against the gods and became self-seeking could no longer endure their sight. He fled from Sekhmet. The Greeks, too, come from the line of a rebel. Aeolus, Dorus, Ion and Achaeus, the ancestors of the Greeks, are the sons and grandsons of that Hellene who, in his turn, is the grandson of Prometheus. Prometheus, the great rebel, is the original ancestor of the Greeks. And now man must come to know that he can no longer endure that dark world of primal forces. So terrifying has it become for him

73

that whoever so much as glances at it is turned to stone. That is the Medusa.

But man has also been given cunning and that mirror of the world which is his intellect; he can use it to catch the reflection of the world and hold it fast. If he, the son of the gods, can approach Medusa as master of this mirror—and he must be a hero to do this, for it is always a terrifying experience—he can overcome her, and out of her will then arise the winged horse of phantasy. And so the true conqueror and master of the horrifying world of night turns out to be: the artist! The primordial world of darkness and dread that threatens man's very existence lies in wait for him everywhere in a work of art. That is what makes every genuine work of art both so breathtaking and so vexing. But now that that world has been tamed and overcome, it can be understood. This is the glorious, liberating feeling of heightened life that comes toward us out of every true work of art.

In those days in Greece, MAN became an artist and thereby laid the foundation for his freedom.

The Temple

How does the Greek give his temple its shape? In other words, how does he experience, visualize and long for the "House of God," the cosmic structure of his own body? And what is his relationship to it?

There is perhaps no clearer way of illustrating the nature of Greece than to compare the Greek temple with the Egyptian one. Such a comparison shows what a gigantic step man had taken when the sun that had settled into the grave in Egypt rose again at the dawning of a new world-day in Greece.

To begin with the most external aspect: The Egyptian temple turned

Plate 17. Medusa Rondanini. Roman copy of the Medusa head on the shield of the statue of Athena in the Parthenon. About 440 B.C. Munich. The frequency of the representation indicates that at that time it must have been an important motif.

inwards—so completely, resolutely and exclusively that from the outside nothing could be seen of it but a smooth, undifferentiated, impenetrable wall and the all-concealing facade of the pylon. The Greek temple turns outwards with the same determination. No one ever enters it but the priest himself. Nothing is concealed in it but the statue of the god. Yet the temple is the garment in which the god manifests himself. The splendor of this building and the richness of its forms all radiate outwards.

The Egyptian temple even projected its strong inward orientation outwards by forcing whoever simply came toward it into a single, predetermined direction, binding him and drawing him hypnotically into itself along its relentless pathway. The figures of the sphinxes—those crouching, immovable guardians of stone—guided him toward it from one side only and kept him from straying even a few steps to the right or left. The same arrangement continued on inside it. The Egyptian temple is a steady procession, a sacred *path.*

The Greek temple simply *stands.* Man can choose the place from which he wants to look at it, in other words, his "standpoint." His eyes—but not only his eyes—are free to move around it from all sides. Of course, it has both a front side and a back one, but hardly anything distinguishes the one from the other. In fact, the frieze that encircles the whole temple between the entablature and the roof is a direct and forceful challenge to walk all around the sanctuary, look at it from all sides and reach around it with one's eyes (Plate 18).

These are only external facts, but they tell us something essential already. The Egyptian "went inside." Pulled in by the high, narrow doorway, he would throw himself into another world, so to speak, just to be overcome there by mighty, superhuman experiences. A flood of sensations would overwhelm him; completely at their mercy, he would be filled with fear and trembling at his total lack of will and feeling of nothingness in their midst.

This is just what the Greek does not want. He wants to stay "outside," confronting, free. His relationship to the world is entirely different. This is a giant step for man to take on the way toward becoming himself—an infinite gain, but at the same time an infinite loss. For even though man in Egypt is less independent, he is much more intimately bound up with

Plate 18. Athens, Theseion. Temple of Hephaestus at the foot of the Acropolis on the ancient Agora. Begun in 449 B.C.

76

the archetypal divine powers from which he then frees himself more and more in Greece. To some, this ability to plunge into primordial forces and overwhelming powers and put oneself completely at their mercy, swimming to keep afloat but never knowing which shore one will be washed up onto, may seem like something higher and worth striving for. Certainly, a person who can still have such experiences is better off than someone whom living feelings no longer touch at all. But in the end what Greece attained is something higher still and leads on further: that man can step up to something and back from it again, keeping whatever distance seems appropriate. The Greek no longer puts himself in the hands of divine powers. He takes the world into his own hands and looks at his new treasure with reverent amazement, holding it closer or farther away so that his admiring eyes can take it in in its entirety. This is how the Greek temple stands in the midst of its surrounding landscape.

It wants to be looked at from the outside, as a magnificent, perfect structure at rest within itself. It wants men's eyes to roam freely around it, touch it, grasp (*herum-greifen*) it and finally con-ceive (*be-greifen*) it.

Here we have one of the archetypal words of ancient Greek culture. *To conceive* is what the Greek longs for more than anything else. It was the Greek who first began to form "concepts" and create a philosophy. Before this there was only the myth, which "gripped" men's souls with its powerful pictures. Man frees himself from the overpowering influence of these pictures through thinking. The Greek sage and the Greek artist both take part in the deed of Perseus in that both of them carry his reflecting shield. This archteypal experience is behind each individual feature that we find so enchanting about Greek architecture.

First of all, there is its marvelously clear organization, which harmoniously keeps the various architectural elements apart by the way it interrelates them: the sacred *foundation*, which bears the image of the god, is particularly emphasized by a few steps leading up to it and the fact of its "elevation"; the *roof* with its heavy horizontality comes down from above, protecting, sheltering, but also weighing down; finally, the supporting *columns* stand in between these with an intensely living verticality, pointing in both directions: receiving and accepting the weight from above and pushing back against the ground. We only fathom what all this meant at the time these temples were first conceived when we realize that there had never been anything like this before. The Egyptian temple was a huge, homogeneous block with an inner space hollowed out of it. And no matter where signs of similar experiences became evident in Egypt, they never matured to the clarity which reached such perfection in Greece with such divine self-assurance.

Finally, there are the *measurements* themselves: the extremely clear relationships of the different parts of the building to each other and the way they meet and fit together so harmoniously. Each temple has its own characteristic dimensions, depending on which god it is intended to house. The temples of Apollo have one kind of proportion, those of Zeus and Hera another, and so on. Here more than anywhere else is where we find an echo of ancient Egyptian wisdom. Remember the pyramids and the correlations of musical, astronomical and mathematical experience. On this basis one could say that each god has a different harmony or a different melody. And yet how different it all is here. This is not the superhuman, magical, primordial power of the cosmic tone that makes the whole of creation tremble. It is the human melody of the *right measure*, or *moderation*:—the great apollonian ideal. These temples could only have been built by a people who called the world a "cosmos," meaning "that which is well-ordered," and for whom this "order" was so important that they applied the same word to the concept of "jewelry" and "decoration" because they never found a better one. The Greek felt that moderation was what made the human being human. The contempt he had for the "barbaros" was the same contempt he had for whoever was immoderate. For that, and not something like "uncultured," is what this word really means. "Barbarians," after all, included the Egyptians and other peoples as well whose cultures the Greeks fully acknowledged.

This, then, is how the temples of the Greek occupied the landscape, the landscape of his soul: beckoning downward to him everywhere from the heights. People could raise their eyes to them from anywhere at all: the peasant in his field, the wanderer on the road, the artisan in his house, the boatman sailing along the coast. Whenever they did so they saw this marvel and drank in clarity, understanding and moderation. For gazing at the temple must have been something like a gentle, barely perceptible communion that was constantly being renewed, an inflowing and a partaking of the substance of the force of that spirit by which man always felt fed, strengthened and confirmed in his humanity again.

But where and how did the Greek encounter this spirit in concrete terms?

If we try to experience the Greek temple as a totality, to take it in completely and arrive at a feeling for it within ourselves, we will get a strong sense of its almost polar duality: on the one hand, the solid temple-core or cella, with its massive walls; on the other, the surrounding wreath of columns (Plate 19). They are like two bodies held together intimately by the roof: a solid, earthy one and one that is more open, airy and porous. It is impossible not to feel how the columns lay themselves like a second, finer body around the first one, how the air breathes around them and washes against them and how they actually play with this element. For the individual columns have not closed themselves off from it behind smooth, round surfaces; they actually take in the air in a kind of breathing process by pulling back from it again and again in their fluting. They are like a fine web with a mysterious melody running through it, flowing around the actual body of the temple. The materiality of this web has nearly dissolved away, for the infinitely lovely vistas of the landscape through the colonnade are a part of this experience too.

As it develops, this web loses its heaviness more and more and is completely permeated with a quiet but all-pervading life. There are no right angles or rigid verticals; swelling and contracting, each column breathes gently within itself.

Now what is the archetypal human experience that led to this whole arrangement? We can see it in a certain group of sculptures that we need to deal with now before taking up the topic of Greek sculpture as such.

Among the clothed figures are certain ones whose garments seem to reveal the body more than they conceal it. One of these is the torso of a goddess (probably *"Aphrodite"*) made in the 4th century and now in Rome. The so-called "Sisters of the Thread of Life," "Goddesses of Fate," or simply *"The Three Fates"* (Plate 20) from the east pediment of the Parthenon and the *"Iris"* from its west pediment could also be mentioned, along with many, many others. The garment is a thin, almost insubstantial veil accompanying the body, surrounding it and nestling up against it everywhere, only to display it more magnificently, like a river flowing uphill. The way it does this is more than masterly technique; it is the expression of a great experience. The people themselves who made these statues must have felt a delicate nestling, shaping, sculpting movement flowing gently and weightlessly all around their bodies, bathing them with something out of which their own bodily form had come.

Plate 19. Parthenon on the Acropolis in Athens. About 440 B.C. Ambulatory between the cella and the surrounding colonnade.

Plate 20. The "Three Fates" from the east pediment of the Parthenon. Together with the other gods, Hestia, Aphrodite and Dione experience with awe the new world-day which dawns as Athena is born from Zeus's forehead. London, British Museum.

Another member of the group of sculptures just mentioned is the altar headpiece usually known as the "Ludovisi Throne" with its relief representation of the *"Birth of Aphrodite,"* the very myth that tells of Aphrodite's emergence from the sea. It is clear from this relief that the sea she came out of could never be located on a map. Both Aphrodite and her servants are wearing garments that are like fine rain. This impression is strengthened by the fact that the two servants are holding another garment loosely stretched between them like a curtain which Aphrodite is rising up behind or out of. She "goes ashore" from that delicate body of formative forces that flows around the earth. One could also say that this is how beauty takes its first steps upon the earth: in the body of man, in the body of the statue, in the body of the temple (Plate 21).

Plate 21. The Ludovisian Throne with the birth of Aphrodite. About 470 B.C. Rome. Presumably not the seat of a throne but an altar top. (What it represents is disputed. It could be an initiation scene).

Its home, however, the world from which it receives its essence, is that other world, the one before the world of the senses. For "Aphrodite" cannot be translated simply by the abstract concept of "beauty." Something of her deeper nature and her secret was still known at the time of the Renaissance. When the Italian humanist, Marsilio Ficino, wrote his book, "On Love or Plato's Symposium," about 1475, he said in it about Aphrodite: "They call his (the angelic spirit's) being Chronos, his life Zeus and his thinking Aphrodite; similarly, they call the world-soul Chronos, Zeus and Aphrodite; insofar as this soul thinks the celestial, they call it Chronos; insofar as it moves the spheres of heaven, Zeus; insofar as it brings about what is down below, Aphrodite . . ." In us as human beings, he goes on to say, it manifests as our two faculties of cognition and procreation. All that is very abstract and stated in a language that has taken its conceptual form from medieval scholasticism. Nevertheless, the essential point is clear: the creative power that can shape a physical body is still experienced as intimately interwoven with the world of divine thinking. Beauty also reveals the deepest thoughts of God. Goethe expressed the same secret in his own characteristic fashion when he said of Greek art that it was "the revelation of secret laws of nature that would have remained hidden without it."

That is what the Greek was longing for and what the Greek temple joyously proclaimed: the "conceiving" of the "secret laws of nature." Egypt had still experienced them as archetypal creative forces in the powerful flow of the primal element. Greece, however, experiences how Aphrodite "goes ashore." Now she reveals herself as beauty. And down from the heights she greets the Hellene from out of every temple. This is the breath that blows through the new "cosmos," bringing joy and freedom.

Sculpture

Sculpture embodies the same laws as the temple. It too proclaims the freeing of the human being and the deep joy of the man who wakes up into this world of experience. For there is nothing else that permeates all its figures, each and every one of them, as much as this.

There is a word which, like a secret, archetypal word, lies on all their smiling lips and slumbers behind their every gesture: *composure*. A composure that maintains itself even in situations where we would be inclined to expect the strongest passion. The *"Eros of Centocelle,"* for example. Isn't Eros a raging god? And yet how calmly this one inclines his beautiful head with a pensive smile. Then there is the *"Satyr"* of Praxiteles. The way he leans, smiling, against the tree makes it hard to imagine that he was ever in a rage. And even the *"Dying Niobid"* suffers death as a quiet parting (Plate 22).

Plate 22. Dying Niobid. About 460 B.C. Rome, Museo delle Terme. Originally probably part of a group (perhaps within a pediment). One of the seven daughters of Niobe who, like her seven sons, were struck down by the avenging arrows of the gods for Niobe's insolent arrogance toward the divine Leto, who had only had two children, Apollo and Artemis.

This is something tremendous. For it means that the human being has learned to master the world of dark, surging emotions and feelings and is no longer their puppet and mindless tool, as he was in Egypt. This is not to say that the Greek was no longer aware of such a world. This composed freedom had to be rewon again and again. It was more a yearning than it was a fulfillment. And yet it flowed into the viewer out of every work of sculpture and had a formative influence on him. Everything that we admire in Greek sculpture is due to this sort of experience.

The Egyptian statue had a rigid orientation, regardless of whether the figure was sitting, standing or walking. With its whole being it looked, walked or moved in a single direction. This means, however, that it was subject to something external to it that pointed it beyond itself. We must never forget that the reason for this was entirely intentional and not due to any technical inadequacy on the part of the artist. In Egypt man was still bound by forces outside him which pointed to something beyond him.

In Greece, however, a kind of sculpture is born that is *at rest within itself.* How all these standing, walking, playing, bending figures enjoy *themselves* as they do these things! What drives them forward or holds them back and gives them their dignity and greatness is not something above or outside them but something within them. They ask us to understand them as figures at rest within themselves who live out their lives in all directions, not just one. They ask us to walk around them and look at them from all sides, feel them within ourselves and experience the totality of their being. Man as a being at rest within himself was born in Greece. This is why Greece is the first real home of *sculpture in the round.*

The clear architectural *organization* achieved in the temples is also evident in the sculptures. How happy all these figures are to have joints, in which their limbs can meet and move freely. People have knees, and the very first Greek statues, such as the famous *"Apollo of Tenea,"* shout this fact out for the whole world to hear (Plate 23)! Later on, this awareness spreads over the whole body until at last there is an experience, not only of the individual limbs and their interplay, but also of the individual muscles and the way they work together.

Plate 23. Apollo of Tenea. One of the many "Kouroi," or young male figures of the Archaic period who were presumably not intended to represent gods, but only young men. About 550 B.C., from the region around Corinth. Munich, Glyptothek.

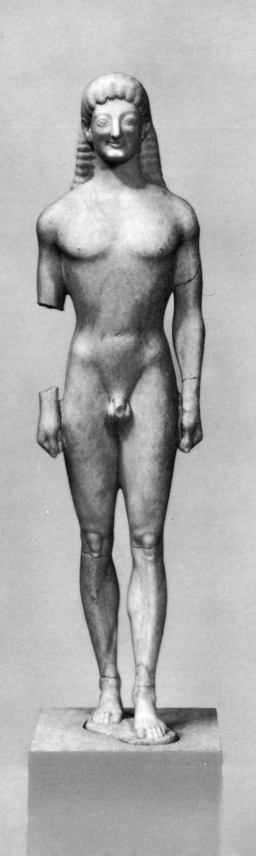

This was not the case in Egypt. From an anatomical point of view, the Egyptian sculptures are admirably "correct," but the fact that they have movable limbs is not the main thing that these pharaohs and gods and all the others experience as they stand or walk or kneel or sit on thrones. What really matters is that this body is the vessel for a feeling that fills it to its outermost limits: a feeling of unity that overpowers the individualities of all the separate parts.

This utterly different way of experiencing the world has such deep roots that it permeates the whole texture of life and even comes to expression in the different political structures of the two peoples. In Egypt the result is the absolute permeation of the whole magnificent organism by the being of the *one* pharaoh; in Greece, it is a democracy that cannot stand to have only a single individual, even a well-meaning one, as its ruler. On the one hand, the overwhelming restriction of everything individualistic through the agency of a single, superhuman being. On the other, the wonderfully free interplay of the individual parts of an organism, organized and working together in accordance with "secret laws of nature."

Another part of this context is the discovery of the *weight-bearing leg* and the *relaxed leg* which the Greeks arrived at in the course of the 5th century. This enabled the figures to free themselves from the ground, in which the Egyptian statues were still deeply rooted. Now they can walk freely over the earth, touch it, release themselves from it, rest on it, push off, overcome gravity—and yet still feel it. This feeling of *relaxation* and its enjoyment is the origin of all those sleeping figures, for example, whose whole being is filled with this wonderful experience.

The rigorous organization of the body and all its parts in Egyptian sculpture is absolute. As with an Egyptian building, one could recognize everything essential about an Egyptian statue by making a cross-section of it. This could not be done with a Greek statue because it is not oriented along a single plane but has each of its various elements—right and left leg, right and left arm, upper and lower body, head, etc.—pointing in a different direction.

The essential feature of Egyptian sculpture was its infinite concentration. All the limbs were drawn in close to the body; it "held itself together" for fear of being "scattered." Otherwise it would have lost the breath of God, which whispered through it and was the essential source of its life. Greek sculpture no longer knows this fear. When we recall such statues as the "*Unguent-Pouring Athlete*," the "*Youth of Antikythera*," who is perhaps a representation of "Paris with the Apple," the "*Apoxyomenos*" and many others, we see how far and how freely they reach or step out into earthly space. But they never lose themselves by reaching out too far. They know enough to stay within "their own" limits. Free of restrictions, they look at us as relaxed, self-contained human beings at rest within themselves.

The works of Greek art are wonderful because what Man himself achieved in Greece is so wonderful. Everything that we have looked at so far can be felt streaming together in a single figure that can lead us even deeper into the background of what was taking place at that decisive hour of human history. It is the statue of a "*Charioteer*" that was found in Delphi. The figure stands firmly and securely erect, calmly looking straight ahead and holding the reins firmly in his powerful, outstretched arms. He is relaxed, self-contained, at rest within himself (Plate 24).

But the full significance of this figure only becomes apparent when we view it in a wider context.

The Battle of the Centaurs

In the middle of the 5th century, at what was perhaps the most significant moment in all Greek history, a particular image suddenly appeared in several different places. It was the myth of the battle of the centaurs and the Lapithae, represented in reliefs at prominent places everywhere: in the west pediment of the temple of Zeus in Olympia, in the metopes of the Parthenon in Athens, in the frieze of the temple of Apollo at Phigeleia, places that were important already because of their very scarcity.

This myth relates how, at the wedding of Pirithous, king of the Lapithae, and Hippodamia, which Theseus was also attending as a guest and friend of Pirithous, the centaurs became so drunk that they attacked the bride and the women of the hosts in order to abduct them (Plate 25). The bride herself had "a lovely figure, the delicate face of a maiden and such beauty that all the guests called Pirithous lucky because of her." In the

battle which followed the Lapithae finally won out, but it was no easy task. The centaurs were killed or had to flee "out into the night."

The centaurs were creatures with a human head and chest growing up out of an animal body. But we must not think of them as nothing but products of a phantastic state of mind, except in the sense of Richard Wagner's Hans Sachs, who says in "Die Meistersinger" that ". . . poetry is only the interpretation of poetic dreams." But even that is not enough. The centaurs really existed, and there is no doubt that many a Greek saw them. But the Greek may have known just as clearly that, as centaurs, they belong to a different sphere of the world than the one we perceive with our outer senses. Nevertheless, they were real enough that battles with them were matters of life and death. The battle with the centaurs really took place, and the reliefs portray a definite historical event that was precisely known.

The centaur is a creature that is still only half human. Part of the human being has yet to be born out of what is still like an animal. In fact, from the pictorial representations we get the impression that what is really in charge of the creature's will is not the human element but the animal one. It is hard to imagine that impulses from the human head or the human heart would be strong enough to rule its whole being. On the contrary: the animal carries the helpless human being wherever it wants to. The centaur is the human being that has not yet become fully human; the forces that surge through it are still the ancient, cosmic, nature-bound ones of instinct that determine the intrinsic nature of the animal.

We will only understand the centaur completely by looking at it against the background of Egypt. We know from history that external factors were at work there too and that the Greeks got much of their deeper wisdom from the Egyptian temple centers that were still in existence at that time. But Greece took what it received from these sources and developed it further in keeping with the stage it had reached in its own evolution. The centaur is a further stage of development in a series of pictures that had begun in Egypt.

Egypt had revered the nature of the animal as something divine and

Plate 24. Bronze statue of a charioteer from Delphi. One of the many consecrated offerings to Apollo and his oracle in Delphi. Pliny reports that after Nero had carried off the 500 most beautiful statues there were still 3000 left. About 460 B.C. Delphi.

superhuman. We have already discussed what was meant by this and to what extent such an attitude was justified: as a distant recollection of a time when man was still passing through the animal stage. That is the first stage.

The second stage was also reached in Egypt and can be recognized in that great, enigmatic image that is something like an epitome of the whole culture: the sphinx. A human head is struggling to escape from the body of an animal. That was Egypt: still crouched down heavily in the animal's horizontal position, and completely devoted to the breath and pulse-beat of overwhelming cosmic forces with by far the greatest part of its being. The new impulse of erectness is only able to become effective as far as the human head, which manages to free itself and attain an upright position.

The centaur is the third stage of this development. Not only the head is born now, but the chest as well, the center of the human pulse and breath. But man is still immersed in the gloom of night. It is true that thinking and feeling have been set free into the human sphere, but the actual forces of the will rise up out of the deep darkness to carry and pull man around wherever they will. The centaur is still more related to the animal than it is to man. The sphinx forces of Egypt are at work in it even more strongly than the human forces of Greece.

From all this one can also see why the centaur is not considered evil or despicable as such. The centaur Chiron was the educator of the great heroes of antiquity and also the wisest of all physicians. From that ancient dream consciousness a kind of knowledge emerges that is deeper and sees much further than the everyday waking consciousness of man. Nietzsche had an intimation of this when he wrote: "O man, pay heed! What does deep midnight say? The world is deep, meant deeper than the day." And especially when it comes to the organic and the forces of life, what this consciousness has to say is inexhaustible. That is why Chiron is the wise healer.

That was long ago. Now, however, the Greek feels this being thrusting its hand out after the most wonderful thing he knows: the beautiful, delicate, maidenly element that he wants to marry. Hippodamia means "horse-tamer." Pirithous is related to the stem of a word meaning "expe-

Plate 25. Abduction of the Bride from the west pediment of the temple of Zeus in Olympia. A centaur reaches for the bride of Pirithous, king of the Lapithae. About 460 B.C. Olympia.

93

rienced," or more particularly, "experienced in earthly matters." Theseus is connected with the stem of a word which means "to put in order." All this, in a nutshell, is the world of Greece. The Greek senses how that other, half-dreaming world of the centaurs is reaching out for the soul of Greece, trying to carry it off.

In the west pediment of the temple of Zeus in Olympia a figure is added to all these that is actually the central figure of the whole composition. It is Apollo (Plate 26), standing in the center with his arm imperiously outstretched, dominating the entire pediment and towering above all the other figures. He is the one who really decides the outcome of this battle, and the Greek feels him to be the source of the force by virtue of which he himself has become *Man* and his soul is able to tear itself away from its dull animal nature. It was also Apollo who killed the dragon, Python, and over his temple in Delphi—built at the very spot where the dragon had fallen into a chasm and was still sending up hot, poisonous, hallucinatory vapors—the words, "Know thyself!" were written.

Apollo is the sun god. But the majestic, bright and mighty celestial body that he makes rise is not only the one that moves across the outer heavens, and the sea that he rises out of every morning is the Aegean only for the outer eye. In reality it is the same sea that gave birth to Aphrodite, and Apollo also makes the sun rise that shines over the heights and depths of the human soul, giving it clarity and wakefulness and calling forth its life. This is that Arcadia where he can be experienced as the Lord of the Muses and the Lord of the Lyre, as he appeared in Hölderlin's mournful lines:

> "Where are you? drunken now, my soul grows dim
> From all delight of you; for just now it was
> That I listened to how, full of golden
> Sounds, the enchanting sun-youth
>
> Played his evening song on his heavenly lyre.
> Forests and hills are resounding all around,
> Yet he has gone to god-fearing people,
> Far away, who honor him still."

Plate 26. Apollo in the midst of the battle of the Lapithae and Centaurs, from the west pediment of the temple of Zeus in Olympia.

Now we can see how the Greek experienced the centaur's defeat: It is the Lord of the Muses who frees the soul from the powers of the deep.

Expressed conceptually, this means that the human being who simply gives himself up to the working of the forces of life remains dull, passionate, immoderate and akin to the animal. Whoever simply shoves these forces aside in favor of the spirit may gain clarity and a measure of morality, but he also becomes a withered intellectual and can never be sure that they will not come back to him some day and exact a terrible revenge. The man who really overcomes them and attains his freedom is the *"muse-filled"* or *artistic human being* who stands in the middle between the other two like Pythia, Apollo's priestess, who sat over the pit out of which the dragon's vapors rose and at the same time received inspiration from the divine forces coming down to her from above. This is man between the animal and God, where the breath of freedom blows that becomes one with a higher necessity. As far from compulsion as from caprice, this freedom lives in obedience to the law, and yet in this very obedience it experiences the greatest and most blissful sense of independence.

This is the miracle of Greece that even today causes human souls to tremble, stirred by the greatness of what radiated from all its temples and statues, its poetry and its people. It is Apollo's magnificent, powerful victory song of the freeing of Man in the artist, echoing far away to the coasts of Italy and Sicily and across the islands to the coasts of Asia Minor, heard still in Macedonia and dying away gently in Egypt.

Man as an artist. All human activity stood under this sign, including the thinking that Greece achieved when it created philosophy. Greece wanted to "conceive." But even thinking was an artistic deed. A thought was not experienced in Greece as an abstract, subjective entity that man "comes up with" himself. Where this was the case, as it was among the Sophists, it was felt to be a mistake. The world of thought was an objective one, as Plato finally expressed this so gloriously in his doctrine of the Ideas or Archetypal Images. In this way we can also see why Socrates felt that the ultimate and most justifiable reason for his violent death was the fact that he had never given in to the voice of the spirit that had often whispered to him, "Socrates, be a musician!" The Greek despised the inartistic person no less than he did the barbarian. If the latter was a threat because of his animallike lack of self-control, the menace of the former was death in the form of intellectual aridity. So Greek philosophy is a verse of Apollo's victory song too, for thinking is another way to feel Apollo's hand as it gently touches the hidden lyre strings of man's being.

Apollo as the guiding spirit of Greece, who makes man the victor in the battle of the centaurs—now we understand why these scenes appear in such prominent places. But why do they suddenly appear at just this moment?

It is the time of the Persian Wars, one of the most terrible and decisive conflicts in the history of the world, a struggle for Greece's very survival, and for a great deal more, in fact. The consequences of a Persian victory would have been inconceivable. The whole of world history would have been different. At any rate, there would have been no such thing as western culture. For this was far more than a political and military struggle; it was a spiritual struggle in the deepest sense of the word. In the Persians we see Asia reaching over toward Europe, and with it that whole world of dull, dreaming, indistinct consciousness that was oriented away from the earth. The centaur was reaching for the glorious soul of Greece and for the soul of Man. The song of victory that rang out after the battles of Salamis and Marathon was again the victory song of Apollo. The Greeks erected a memorial to the fighters who had fallen at Thermopylae. Its stirring lines breathe something of the magnitude of this hour in the history of the world:

"Traveller, when you come to Sparta, announce to the people
that you have seen us lying here dead by command of the law."

These men knew that not one of them would return from the battle they were about to enter, and yet they willingly took it on. There seemed to be no better way to honor them than by making their immortal resolve known to the world in lines that contain no slightest trace of heroism but only the stern phrase, "by command of the law." But the law they were obeying was greater than any thought up by human beings. The melody of these two lines with their open secret of the celebration of a super-human victory is the melody of Apollo.

This is not to say that the Greeks somehow "symbolized" their wars with the Persians in their portrayals of the battles with the centaurs. The inner connection is much deeper. This hour is one of the very few in human history when we see man rising directly into the spiritual world.

It has been a never-ending source of amazement that the Greeks were able to create such an overwhelming abundance of their most magnificent works of art "on the side," so to speak, in the same decades in which they had to engage all their forces in this terrible struggle to simply survive. But it remains an enigma only so long as the attitude persists that art is something "alongside" of life. The truth is that the actual struggle for life during those decades, the original "battle of the centaurs," was not fought near Salamis, Marathon or Thermopylae at all but in the studios of the sculptors and on the building sites of the temples. That was where man experienced his victory over the centaurs and his consequent liberation again and again and where he could hear the soft melody of Apollo in its overwhelming beauty, clarity and harmony. A study of the inner reality of human evolution shows that those were the places where the great victory was achieved.

What about the Persian Wars themselves? They were the external "precipitate" or "condensation" of spiritual forces that had originally battled with each other in the soul of man, which at that time felt more at home in Greece than anywhere else. That battle became a struggle that engaged the whole being of man and even, we are tempted to say, the entire earth.

This is one of the moments in history which Schelling apparently had in mind when he made his demand that history should gradually become meta-history, just as physics becomes meta-physics. It is one of those moments when inmost and outermost reality unite, as history rises to the level of mythical greatness and the guiding spirit of human destiny emerges from his customary obscurity. For once, his unfathomable artistic web becomes so transparent that he himself and his mighty form can be felt behind it.

This whole train of thought began with the figure of the "*Charioteer.*" The connection may now be clear. The charioteer is the fourth stage in that sequence of pictures, the first three of which were the divine animal, the sphinx and the centaur. In the charioteer this development is complete. Man has pulled away from the animal and has released the animal from himself. He stands outside it now, awake, self-disciplined and in control. The charioteer has conquered the centaur. And the *true* charioteer, the archetype who stands behind each of these images, is Apollo. He is the heavenly, divine charioteer who leads the sun upward with his glorious team of horses; he is the one the Greek experienced *within himself* as the divine power of his Ego.

This is the significance of that picture which finally became an archetypal image of the Greek personality: the man who lets himself be carried along by the animal's great strength, yet holds the reins firmly in his hands; standing there, free and glorious, he has neither killed the animal nor pushed it away but tamed it and made it serve him. The chariot races at the Olympic games must have been experienced in this deeper sense also. They were not just "sporting" events but elemental human experiences as well. The exuberance that filled the Greek when he saw the teams of horses racing along through the stadium; the animal's strength, unfettered but securely controlled by its magnificent superior who had it completely "in hand"—all this was a confirmation of the charioteer in man himself. Again and again this picture engraved itself deeply in the Hellenic soul. Plato uses it as an archetypal picture of the soul's activities.

But in the end what was experienced there was always the radiant spirit behind the rising sun of Greece. "The charioteer" means: the rise of *Man*.

Moira

One could say that the Greek is "*gelassen*," whereas the Egyptian was "*gefesselt*" by his gods. If we take both these words in their double meanings,* we understand man's infinite gain, but also his infinite loss. For the Egyptian's "captivation" actually means that the gods still stood, great and glorious, before his gaze, drawing him to themselves, and only to themselves, with their magic power. The Greek's "composure," on the other hand, means that the gods had forsaken him and left him on his own. How much, for instance, does the Greek still know about the world on the other side of the portal of death, which was so wide open for the Egyptian?

The human being "relaxed," "at rest" or "confined" within himself is born. No matter how far he may reach out into space, he never reaches out beyond "his" space; he always stays "within himself." But he also no longer reaches out into that other, greater world in which the Egyptian

*Translator's note: *Gelassen* means "left," "left to oneself" or "left free," but also "calm," "composed" or "moderate." *Gefesselt* means "fascinated" or "captivated," but also "fettered."

still felt completely at home. Whether we think of the so-called *"Idolino,"* the famous *"Praying Boy"* with his arms raised high or the *"Praying Youth"* in the Vienna Hofmuseum, they all remain within their humanness, and it is doubtful whether they ever really touch the god they are reaching out to. This is how far the gods had withdrawn, so far that man was already beginning to doubt whether they even existed.

Man is now completely alone upon his earth. But he is willing to shoulder this destiny and to carry it along with everything connected with it. The overwhelming expression of this experience is *the Greek column.*

It has often been considered one of the most significant creations of Greece, perhaps the most significant one of all. And here, too, there is a point at which art reveals the secret of how deep a human experience it is really an outgrowth of.

On the Acropolis in Athens there is a small hall, built on to the austere structure of the Erechtheum. Its roof does not rest on columns but on statues of maidens: the *"Porch of the Maidens"* (Plate 27). This structure is not just some artistic whim. This is the only time that the beings who are normally completely hidden inside have stepped out and become visible. For there is actually something soul-like enclosed inside each column. These columns are able to be shaped this way because power to support has come into existence within the human being himself. This is the artistic experience behind the Greek column and its gradual transformation from the older, purely vegetative plant column: supportive power. Serenely growing toward what lowers itself from above as a weight, then, when it arrives, widening out,holding oneself ready, receiving, shouldering, carrying.

The Greeks were the first people capable of having such an experience. For it could only come about in a portion of humanity that had become so separate from the gods that it had a destiny. Before that, men had no destiny to face, just as plants and animals have none. Everything that happened simply occurred, and its source was the world of the gods. Even in Egypt, where man felt so deeply in debt to the world because he was seeking his selfhood, the concept of guilt was still unknown. Egypt had nothing comparable to the Greek Moira, to Clotho, Lachesis and Atropos, the three fates, or to the Erynnies, the goddesses of revenge.

Plate 27. Porch of the Maidens, Erechtheum with the six caryatids on the Acropolis in Athens. About 415 B.C.

Not until man had become a self, "left to himself" as he was in Greece, did he experience destiny breaking in upon him from a world of deep darkness. Man becomes guilty, and out of guilt destiny is born. But man is ready to take it on and "bear" it, in order that in the end a reconciliation with the world order may again take place. So it is that the same human beings who invent the column also become the inventors of the *tragedy*.

What became gesture in the Greek column shows its face in another branch of art as well: the *burial stele* (Plate 28). To appreciate fully what was accomplished here in human terms, we must keep the Greek's attitude toward death in mind. How he loved the earth! As for the beyond, he certainly knew that there was a world and an existence beyond the grave. But how uncertain it all was. In that realm the soul felt like nothing more than a shadow. That is why Homer exclaims: "Better a beggar in the upper world than a king in the realm of shades!" This is how the Greek felt. Here on the earth he was at home, and death was the final farewell to all that he loved so well, the threshold of no return into the uncertain grayness. But what does he *do*?

We could understand if he put up a fight or vehemently complained, or if outbursts of despair were written there. Instead, we find only bearing and calm acceptance. The most one permits oneself is a feeling of tender sadness. How gently the held hands separate. How calmly the youth has laid aside his weapons and sits there now with cheek in hand, looking back toward his short upward path. How full of pain, how tenderly and without complaint the eyes of the lovers meet once more for one last, deep look.

It is a moving sight. A degree of human dignity has been attained here that can hardly be surpassed. Only the fewest really died that way, or were allowed to. But it was the ideal, and now and then it was also achieved. A case in point is the death of Socrates, a decisive event in which the gesture of the Greek column proved its true worth. Another successful test of this attitude took place whenever young men went off to battle, singing and adorned as if for some festive occasion. Apollo's victory song can be heard resounding through these songs, too.

The *Centaur* is defeated and *Man the Charioteer* is born.

Plate 28. Attic burial stele from Rhamnus. The dead young woman bids farewell to her husband as he ponders the riddle of this stroke of destiny. About 330-320 B.C. Athens, National Museum.

Wondrous Interlude

The linear development from Egypt to Greece becomes apparent in *archaic Greek art*. The stern restraint of Egyptian art with its rules of frontality and symmetry is still at work in it, but the breath of liberation is already beginning to stir from within.

A thousand years earlier, something happens once again that is like a distant prelude to Greece itself, a prelude that from the outside does not seem like one of the roots of Greek culture at all. This is the world of *Crete*—a whole world in itself. We can only appreciate its historical importance properly by seeing it as a partly playful, but absolutely essential interlude in the great symphonic unfolding of world history. And yet, far off in the distance, we can unexpectedly hear already the motif of the next great movement.

Actually, this world did not produce great art at all, and yet it exuded a certain charm from the moment it began to rise up out of the ground again. It has no great architecture either: no temples, just palaces, and even these seem more like natural growths than like products of conscious planning, as when a tree shoots out new sprouts in all directions. There is also no great sculpture, only a few small figurines. But there are vases, weapons and utensils of remarkable beauty, as well as paintings on the palace walls that give glimpses of an enchanting way of life. No matter what part of it these pictures show, this life is like a dance that takes hold of everything that lives.

The impression arises that this culture sought to express itself less in things that people made than directly in the way they lived. Its people led blissful lives of dreamlike surrender to the great powers of existence and yet, as dreamers, they became a stage on which gods performed deeds of great significance. And, since we know that the language on their clay tablets that for so long seemed indecipherable is none other than Greek, we can also tell which gods they were.

Among the many and diverse pictures of that age, three groups stand out as especially impressive: the picture of the *dancers*, the *goddess* or priestess with snakes in her upraised hands and, finally, the pictures of the *bull games*. There must have been a kind of bull game in Crete in which the aim was not to kill the bull. Instead, whoever faced the bull would grab its horns, swing himself up on it and, with a somersault over its back, jump into the arms of a waiting comrade.

The only way to look at what all these pictures point to is to see them as a prelude to what was discussed in the section, "The Battle of the Centaurs," and in connection with the image of the "Charioteer." It appears most clearly and strikingly in the image of the bull-grappling games just mentioned. Man and animal—in Egypt this relationship is still clearly experienced from the viewpoint of the animal as a divine being. Gods are seen to be at work in the animal's total openness and self-surrender. The pure being of the divine, cosmic forces in all their original power resounds to man through the animal, which is still its most perfect instrument, made by and for these very sounds. In Greece the scales are clearly tipped in favor of man. Man overcomes the animal and with it all unconscious, natural drives and instincts. He has no other choice if he is to find his own true nature. By the time of Crete man had gained some weight and the scales were balanced. Man does not fight the animal, but plays with it and overcomes it through his play. These are pictures of actions that have a religious or ritualistic character. In its modern, conceptual form their meaning would be that man confronts the divine powers. He must summon up all his courage to do this, for the powers are enormously strong and stand ready to destroy the very core of his being. But first there is an "upswing," through which he is lifted up and carried beyond himself by just this force, which is greater than his own. In the end he lands on his own feet again, elated and unharmed (Fig. 9).

We find these powers of the deep represented again and again, as plants and animals from the depths of the ocean or as flowers sprouting

Fig. 9. Bull game. Fresco from Knossos (restored).

105

out of the dark soil of the earth. But they always seem to have been dipped in the same element that is the medium of the bull-grappling games, so to speak, and in which this wonderful, victorious equilibrium is at home: dance and music. Again this is an anticipation of Apollo, the Lord of the Muses, who will appear as the charioteer of all charioteers in Greece.

The statues of the goddesses or priestesses with snakes in their upraised arms are expressions of the same motif: O man, raise the powers of the dark depths up into the light, and they will become the powers of healing. (The motif is very similar to that of the "uplifted" serpent in Numbers 21 and John 3:14.) It is a mystery-prelude to the deed of Perseus.

In fact, the whole Cretan culture is a prelude, experienced and represented by a form of consciousness that is still dreaming. One cannot fail to hear this in the *architecture* of its great palaces. The most striking thing about them is their total lack of symmetry. This means that there is no experience of a central axis as something firmly fixed. This middle element is what one lives in in dance and play. But it seems that in Crete it is only experienced as something that takes hold of man in these moments of "upswing" as if coming from somewhere above him—and then lets go of him again. The ego-quality has not yet been born in this culture; everything is still in a sort of pre-birth state.

The same is true of the second most striking feature of this architecture, namely, the columns that have no base, are very narrow at the bottom and gradually widen out toward the top. They grow upwards like plants that spread out in the light; what they do *not* do is stand there like human beings awakened to their own earthly existence and ready to bear whatever burden is imposed on them. And yet they are already an indication of what will come later in the form of the Doric column.

In Crete the folk spirit of Greece was still dreaming. There is no doubt that this element is what ensouled the whole of Cretan life. Its language is the one the people there spoke, and the Greeks themselves were aware of this; it was from Mount Ida in Crete that Zeus came over to Greece to set up his rule. In Crete itself this strong, young child of the gods was still dreaming in the womb of the times. His hour had not yet come. The mighty spirit of Egypt was still in power.

In Crete the god who wore the form of a bull and bore Europa on his back was dreaming. That was what made his discovery so sensational. He was dreaming all these wondrous shapes in the souls of men.

The wonderful thing about this interlude is the way we can almost see the guiding spirit of Greece at work in it, preparing for the hour of its birth. For when, in it, the sun of the new age rises at the birth of the Charioteer, what this spirit has to reveal is very, very great.

The Path of the Sun God

Once again we must look back to Egypt. Whenever the Egyptian felt the divine being of the sun, the picture that came to his mind was not a chariot but a boat, an image connected with the element of water, just as the former is connected with the solid earth. *The path of the sun god leads from the sea to the solid land.*

This, in its deepest sense, is the path of man from Egypt to Greece. Egypt was still filled with a flood of surging feelings. To the Egyptian they seem endless, overwhelming and alive, and he feels them pouring out primal forces of life. But man himself finds nothing in them to hold on to. Greece is where he takes his first steps on solid, earthly land. There he can stand, secure and composed. He goes his own way. It may be full of thorns; his feet may often bleed; it may often lead him into wilderness and desolation—no matter. Man keeps to his path, for the Lord of the Sun has gone before him. He follows His call. This is the innermost secret of the history of mankind from Egypt to Greece.

The pathway from sea to land, however, is also the way of Christ. What are the most important stations of the way as we find it in the gospels? First of all, the Baptism in the *waters* of the Jordan, where the spirit of Christ descends into Jesus of Nazareth. In Jesus this spirit then goes ashore, onto the *land*, and walks about the earth. After this He goes with His disciples into the *house* of the Last Supper; the Crucifixion, Burial and Resurrection are only a heightening of this experience of the "house" into cosmic dimensions. The path finds its fulfillment on the *mountain* of the Ascension (see *Beitrage zum Verständnis des Evangeliums* (*Studies in the Gospels*), unpublished manuscript by Lic. E. Bock). These, then, are the stages of the path of Christ: out of the water onto the land, into the house and onto the mountain.

107

It is the same path that Christ calls men to follow. The disciples are called from the sea onto the land, and they go with Christ along His earthly path, into the house and out again onto the mountain.

This is not the place to go into these scenes in great detail. Their significance for man is the same as the one we have arrived at on the basis of our studies of the history of art so far: they are stages in the evolution of human consciousness.

Christ today is imprisoned in a book which has become sealed and incomprehensible as well. Wherever people speak of Him at all, it is only the three years of His life depicted in this book they talk about. But the time has come to break these seals and attain an understanding of the cosmic being of the Christ and His mighty journey through the centuries. In this way we will come to see that what the gospels give us is not just the report of three years in the life of a divinely pure human being but, at the same time, the history of *man*. They are a record of the destinies of the guiding spirit of all humanity. These three years are the very core of world history, containing in an incredibly condensed form the essence of everything that has already taken place and will continue to take place for millennia to come. From the opposite point of view, world history is the grandiose unfoldment of what is contained in this one archetypal image over thousands of years.

The deeds and sufferings of Christ have been written, but not only on a few sheets of paper. They have been inscribed into history itself, into the hearts of men, and the history of art is a faithful record of what those hearts have experienced. Novalis once wrote: "Who ever said the Bible is a finished work?" The history of art is also a gospel, and it is not one to be taken lightly.

Behind Re and Apollo a Greater One comes into view, the One who was able to say of Himself: "Before Abraham was, I am." What we have considered up to now is only the first stage of His pathway. Later on we will have to show how the following stages—the house and the mountain —are also indelibly inscribed in the history of art. But perhaps it is already possible at this point to have an inkling of the experience the great Baptizer had beside the Jordan as the time dealt with in this chapter was drawing to its close—that John who, before he ever saw Him, had felt with an inner trembling the step of the Approaching One:

"One is coming . . ."

V

THE TRIUMPHAL ARCH

The Character of Hellenistic, Late Roman and Early Christian Art

The great age of Greek art comes to an end in the same years in which the political independence of the country collapses. (We would be inclined to regard the latter more as a result of the former than as one of its causes.) But what had once blossomed in such magnificence nevertheless remained an ideal that was influential for many centuries to come, long after the land of its birth had become a desolate place of no importance and the names of its gods had nearly been forgotten. The whole of the Middle Ages is still overshadowed by the spirit that had once found its expression in the art of Greece. Even after the dawn of the modern period a long time passes before the later after-effects of that earlier period are entirely replaced by something new.

Shortly after the campaigns of Alexander, and not without an inner connection with them, a "dissolution of form" set in. Everywhere a great unrest broke out which grew and grew as the centuries went by. It invaded the quiet melody of the lines, burrowed deeply into the ever more passionate gestures, swelled and collected in the limbs of sleeping forms, drove individual figures together into tense, dramatic groups, broke out in feeling and pathos and whispered secretly in the now deepened shadows of the reliefs. Everywhere something ineffable was in the air.

This was the rise of the so-called "Hellenistic Baroque." The term is not unjustified, for although the "actual" Baroque of a later age is considerably different from what we see taking shape now, both styles share something without name or measure, an irrational, cosmic element that invades humanity and seeks expression in these forms.

It is the time when the mysteries become part of everyday life in an unprecedented way. This was especially true of the mysteries of the East, which were now more accessible than ever. A regular flood of mysteries took place. Occult knowledge, which was no longer safely hidden in its proper place by reverence and awe but had long since been only half concealed, began to tempt the souls of men by entering their now lustful consciousness. The heavy breath of the Orient is everywhere. All the cults and mysteries which once sheltered the cosmic secrets of the processes of life are now dragged out of their former sacred seclusion in a quite particular way.

This process becomes even more intense as Rome extends its rule over the whole Mediterranean area, becomes the center of the world and establishes the cult of the divine Caesar.

Rome, too, although it has its roots in darker and more impenetrable depths, is a part of that world which knows man now only as an isolated individual, abandoned by the primordial powers of the cosmos. The only difference was that what in Greece had led to the creation of philosophy and such magnificent works of art led in will-oriented Rome to the creation of law and a powerful state. Under the influence of the Egyptian mysteries, now "demonized" and no longer in step with the times, those forces grew stronger and stronger which, from the beginning of Roman history on, had been active as pure will to power. Not only did they seize the young forces of human intelligence, thereby creating an actual "politics" for the first time in human history; they also took hold of the ancient magical forces of the East and used them for their own ends as well. The fratricide with which the history of Rome begins and the power of the she-wolf that suckled Romulus and Remus work on throughout the whole of Roman history.

The image of the wolf is very ancient. The Germanic peoples knew it too as the son of Loki, the cosmic power who is the enemy of the sun, threatens it at every eclipse and finally devours it at the Twilight of the Gods.

Roman rule is the great Twilight of the Gods: an eclipse of the spiritual sun that encompasses the whole history of the world. For the fact that at that time more temples were built, more idols were erected, more sacrifices made and more cultic rites performed than ever before is a clear sign that men were no longer filled with the power of the older, simpler gods.

What is true for religion is also true for art—how could it be other-

110

wise? To be sure, an extensive art industry develops, so extensive that one is almost tempted to speak of mass production, but only a few art works worthy of the name appear, and when they do, their origin is Greek. What is really new and peculiar to Rome, however, speaks in a clear and unmistakable language.

The nature of the new human experience that characterizes a particular culture shows up not only in its artistic style but also in what kinds of objects it chooses to depict. Egypt chose only *graves* and *temples*. Greece included something new: the *theater*. The theater stood originally on some sacred spot set aside for the gods, where it could deal with man and his destiny, his guilt and its atonement. Man was the center of attention. What does Rome add to this? First of all, the *Circus*, which is a metamorphosed theater. Then come the great buildings known as *Thermae*, or public baths. Finally, there is the *Forum*, which is something like a whole new kind of "sacred" area. All these things are expressions of the great new step man is taking on the path away from the gods and toward himself and the earth. The power he subjects himself to at the Forum and for which the Forum is built is the state. Before it, man counts for nothing as far as his eternal being is concerned; he is important only as a citizen, or "civis." The public baths are buildings dedicated to the comfort of this "civis." The huge circuses, however, are monuments to all the dark forces in the abysses of the human soul which were nurtured there. In Greece all artistic creation had had but one basic purpose: the praising of the gods; now it serves only the earthly human being. Art becomes decoration, in every respect.

There is one more thing that Rome produced: the *Triumphal Arch.* Here, more than anywhere else, is where Rome speaks. It is Rome's major form of "self-expression." What it means, however, lies at a much deeper level than the one its accidental connection with a war fought and won at some particular moment of time would suggest (Plate 29).

How these arches stand there in their solid, concentrated mass! Ready to defy eternity, filled with an unrelenting will to power, weighing down the earth as if in them the marching of the legions had contracted into a single gesture. This is how they preserve the fact that someone once entered the city—from far away—as the conqueror of a new land which he had won over for the Empire and to which he had brought the "Roman" form of peace.

It is hard to go too far in picturing to ourselves how magnificent these

111

triumphal entries were, especially since in the provincial cities the mere arrival of Caesar's image was an occasion for great festivities. "A fanfare of trumpets announced them. A long procession of soldiers marched ahead of the richly decorated image-bearer. The crowd moved toward them with torches and incense to give it a festive reception." What a reception they must have given Caesar himself! For he was a man who had broken through the limits of ordinary human existence: by having himself illegally initiated into the mysteries by force, he had made himself into the vessel of a spirit being greater than a man. As a consequence of these unlawful procedures, the spirit that "possessed" may well have been a "dark" one. At any rate, he was experienced as a god and received like one.

The god who has become a man has entered his city—this is what the monumentality of these unique structures is proclaiming. Just this "entrance" and nothing more: not that a race of people has been subdued or the power of the state extended, only the fact that the man who accomplished this has "entered."

This man, of course, had not come in to lay down his life or to be laid into the grave of the earth so that the earth might "grow light again." His weight on the earth was heavy.

If one assumes that the Mystery of Golgotha was an event of cosmic proportions, it at least makes sense to see in these triumphal arches of the Caesars something like a dark counter-image of that other "entrance." Naturally, this was not a conscious plan. It simply happened—on the one hand, in such a way that the whole earth trembled in the dreaming depths of the human soul from the might of this event: His entrance; and, on the other hand, that the Caesars, whose own forcible initiations into the mysteries had made them experienced in the use of magic, also forced a distortion of that experience up out of the depths, seating themselves in the place that was meant for someone else.

It must have been about this time that the altar "to the unknown God" was erected in the marketplace in Athens. In the souls of the people then there may have been many more such altars than we normally imagine. The unrest in anticipation of the coming God was very deep, although His name was still unknown.

Plate 29. The Arch of Titus in Rome. Triumphal arch erected about 70 A.D. on the Forum Romanum to commemorate the victory of Titus over the Jews.

113

Then young Christianity emerged from its catacombs and became a decisive force in the shaping of the new culture. Gradually, new developments of the previous centuries that had once seemed so enigmatic became transparent and revealed their true significance as they came together to form a new and orderly world. A new God has arisen. He is becoming active, not through some teaching but through direct experiences of His reality. The art of this period shows this very clearly, for people use it to express their deepest premonitions. Even those who knew nothing of the new "teaching" or were only dimly aware of His coming created forms which, as we now see, are perfect expressions of what people who had consciously experienced this God would feel the urge to say.

The buildings of early Christianity, the *basilica* as well as the more circular structure with its central dome or cupola, are the immediate and most succinct expression possible of everything that is dawning in man as a new and powerful world of experience. What is so new about this world, as compared to what had found such pure forms in the world of Greece?

First of all, the fact that the temples of this God turn inward again, enclosing an inner space. In this way they somehow continue the development that began in the temples of Egypt. One experiences them, however, not so much by going inside them as by being inside them. Large, unpretentious spaces of infinite solemnity open up. But that is actually not quite the way to describe it, for what people find when they enter these buildings is not "space" in the normal sense at all. A better term for it might be "hyperspace" ("*Überraum*"), because the space it feels like is actually more cosmic than human. This experience has no relation to external dimensions. Even in the smallest buildings it can be quite overwhelming. It completely fills the long hall of the basilica as much as it does a building of the central type (Plate 30).

The *basilica*, which was destined to be the major influence on the future development of western architecture, makes the expression of this feeling, created first by spatial proportions, even more impressive through the uniform, continuous succession of columns which support

Plate 30. Ravenna. Interior of San Apollinare in Classe. Three-aisled basilica without transept. Dedicated to the martyred bishop St. Apollinaris, who stands in the apse mosaic beneath the cross of precious stones surrounded by 99 stars. About 540 A.D.

the wall of the nave and stream toward the apse, where the experience reaches a tremendous climax. In the central type of building (Plates 31 and 32) the expression is enhanced by spaces towering one above the other. Both structures proclaim the meeting of man and God. The longitudinal structure of the basilica stresses more the inner movement of man toward God, the central type more man's quiet resting within God's mighty realm. Always, however, they are born from the experience of God's tremendous reality and substance. As the final and highest intensification of all this, both use the *mosaic*. Its glittering, mysterious glow covers the walls and especially the vaulting of the apse; to be more precise, we should say that it breaks through these and dissolves them. For what breaks through everywhere is spacelessness; through the mosaic the physicality of the building suddenly disappears in the presence of figures from a superhuman world. Sternly they look at us, or on beyond us into another eternity, emerging from their infinite, golden background without ever leaving it.

In the midst of it all: not the picture of a god, but the altar, where again and again the miracle of transformation takes place by means of which the god walks on the earth, thereby entering the world of the earth time after time. Usually, however, the altar stood under what was called the *Triumphal Arch.* At this point it makes no difference how old this term for the arch that separates the apse from the main hall of the church is, nor whether people were consciously connecting with the Roman tradition when they gave the arch this name (although anything else is hard to imagine). The point is that it, too, is the expression of the experience that someone is "entering" through an arch. The pictures on its inner surface say as much, if it were not clear enough already. It may be that the great Benedictus ("Blessed is he who comes . . .") which was sung at the moment of the Transformation was not yet part of the Mass, which we have to think of as still being relatively simple; nevertheless, it was already resounding in the hearts of the people. Through these great rooms it resounds, too.

The Christian basilica is a characteristic shape that decisively influenced the evolution of western architecture for thousands of years. For a long time the question of where it comes from was one of the great rid-

Plate 31. Ravenna, San Vitale, exterior. Foundation stone laid in 526 A.D. Consecrated in 547 A.D.

116

dles of art history. Is it a new and original creation of early Christianity, or are there earlier versions of it? Today this question has probably been answered beyond all doubt, surprising as this answer may be.[10] It is not a new creation, but the handed-down form of a building which in essence had the same external features, namely, the great hall in which Caesar held his formal receptions. The earliest predecessor of this was, in turn, the palace of the pharaoh Merneptah (1234-1225), one of the Ramessides. It thus has its origin in a time when the divine kingship of the pharaohs had already become the servant of governing powers strongly influenced by magic.

From an external point of view, the question seems to have been resolved; in reality it has only become a much deeper one. It will simply not do to try to explain the connection by saying that God has placed His throne in the throne room of His bitterest foe, who in the meantime has been defeated. If the form of the basilica had not been the "right" one in a higher sense, it would not have been preserved for so many centuries. We should rather say that, as in the case of the Triumphal Arch, what Caesar usurped here was something that was actually the property of all humanity and was meant for something completely different.

This becomes even clearer when we look once more at the relationship between the basilica and the Greek temple. What immediately meets the eye is that the former is the latter turned inside out. What was outside in the case of the temple, namely, the columns that surrounded it in such a living way, has now come inside. The inner part, however, the solid wall of the temple-core or cella, has become the outer wall. This means that what the Greek had still experienced "in his surroundings"—the living world of divine creative thoughts, the formative forces of the spirit— is now experienced within. But there is more. The altar, which had stood outside in front of the temple, has come inside along with these other things and has taken over the spot formerly occupied by the image of the god. This image itself, however, is no longer a shining, three-dimensional sculpture blissfully at rest within itself, but a flat picture on the inside surface of the apse, "appearing" as if from out of some non-spatial realm. Often it is not even a picture of the God, but only a symbol of Him for whom the human figure was but a garment.

Plate 32. Ravenna, San Vitale, interior. Central type building on an octagonal ground plan with ambulatory and gallery.

This house is a house of God, not just an assembly hall for some congregation (what an error of a god-forsaken time!). But the God for whom this house was built does not live in it. He only has a place there, the altar on which, again and again, He takes on physical form. He is experienced dynamically in a living, dramatic process. The reason why the congregation, too, can even be in this room is that He becomes alive "inside," perhaps not yet within each individual person, but within the community of human beings as a whole. It is really this group—the congregation—that calls Him in.

The Christian feeling about life and the world, which emanates from the evangelists' tales of the sudden appearances of the Risen One "among them," "when the doors were shut," lives on in this architecture today. The divisive power of the world of space is gone; spacelessness breaks in, as does the light, the unbearable light that blinded Paul on the road to Damascus. This is the open heaven into which the martyrs marched through the midst of their terrible tribulations, singing their hymns and wearing a heavenly glow on their shining faces.

It is clear that this world is a very different one from that of Greece. Its structural elements and forms were developed within the Greco-Roman world, but they were not put to use here until after their original unity had been completely destroyed so that they could become the expression of an entirely different content. What these new structures celebrate is not the joy of comprehending something, but the incomprehensible itself; not the harmony of "right measure," but what cannot be measured at all; not the quietness of being self-contained, but the "invasion" of its quietness by another level of reality. We are forced to ask whether Greece's great achievements have not been lost again after all, overpowered by something boundless, nameless and unfathomable.

This entire period from the 3rd century B.C. to the 4th century A.D. noisily proclaims the trembling of the earth, the shattering of a world by the entrance into it of a being whose approach and presence can be experienced but not fully understood or coped with. The times themselves herald this being as a tremendous cosmic reality, whether they feel it as a source of deep disquiet or as a source of bliss.

On the other hand, is there not something like a gentle beginning of a future will to comprehend in the very fact that these overwhelming spaces have already been embraced and taken hold of? This can also be felt in the fact that very soon organizing forces intervene. In the basilica, these forces bring a rhythmic order into the flowing movement of columns and pillars toward the apse by alternating these supports. (In the central type of building the same results are achieved in a different way.) This will is also alive in the creative forces which soon grow upwards and seek to encompass the entire space by spanning a vault around it.

Of course, it has not all been mastered yet. It is more a sign that a task has been given than that it has actually been carried out. Meanwhile, still unaware of their mission and dreaming in their myths, other peoples are gradually maturing who, with their youthful forces, will one day take up again what began so magnificently in Greece: the peoples of the North. But this legacy has now been increased by the tremendous fact *that the God has entered.*

This becomes the task that the whole Middle Ages will then struggle to resolve: the comprehension of the incomprehensible.

VI

THE CATHEDRAL

On the History of Medieval Art

Nowhere are the art and spirit of the Middle Ages expressed as clearly and as accurately as they are in the concept, "cathedral." Towering above the everyday life of men, it nevertheless stands in the midst of it, bringing the tremendous reality of God down into the world of men, which seems so insignificant in the face of this reality and yet is so exalted by it. The cathedral's glorious architecture encompasses all the individual arts, for outside its sphere there was no great sculpture or painting or great music, and no poetry or drama outside the mystery-drama of the mass. The cathedral embraces them all as a synthesis of the arts in the highest sense of the word. As a result, it is an expression of both the Una Sancta, or One Holy Christian Church, and the Holy Roman Empire of the German Nation; it is filled with a sense of life that knows itself to be at rest within a great and holy unity of the world.

A world, however, in which the miracle is at home and which includes the miracle as its most essential element. The miracle is both the source of this world's life and the center of its activity. The cathedral itself can hardly contain the miracle, and yet it is the central mystery around which the cathedral rises: the Romanesque, more purely and naturally so, built as it is right into the breath of cosmic spaces; the Gothic, folding itself around this center more tenderly and fervently.

This, then, is how it stands there: outwardly defiant, powerfully erect with the vigor of a knight; inwardly tender, concealing the infinite with the humility of a saint. This is medieval man.

The cathedral developed slowly, through an apprenticeship of many centuries. The starting point of this development was the early Christian basilica. The final result shows why it was the basilica that assumed this

122

role rather than the building of the central type, which itself had such a great influence on the architectural development of the East. Inherent in the basilica, though still largely hidden, was its element of drama, its ability to express events and changes. Here and there the quiescent form of the central type was also used in the West, of course, but primarily for baptisteries and funerary chapels—spaces in which man stood at the boundary of the cosmos, leaving it or entering it again. But the major influence on the development of western architecture was the longitudinal structure with its three principal elements: its flowing movement toward and away from the apse; the striving of its whole layout in narthex, atrium and basilica toward a definite goal; and the gently intimated polyphony of the different heights and widths of the nave and aisles.

The roots from which the cathedral drew the strength to transform this original cell reach far and deep into the past. Greece and Rome, the Celtic West, the Byzantine East with the gentle breeze of the Orient wafting through it, and also Islam, have all contributed to its rise. But the richest root was without a doubt the young Germanic North which now, in the cathedral, began to awaken to its own potential.

It would be fascinating to describe how one element after another is formed through the centuries and added to the others. But all of that together would not yet be the cathedral. For the cathedral is more than the simple sum of its parts, and this "more," which is outwardly so insignificant, is what makes the cathedral into a being; it finally bursts in at a single moment, taking hold of all the individual elements and adapting them to itself. This took place about the year 1000, when *St. Michael's* was built in *Hildesheim* (Plate 33) as the first example of the Romanesque style as well as the first work of real artistic perfection. Suddenly, all the uncertainty so evident in the buildings of the previous centuries is gone, and the miracle of the structure resounding out of itself has taken place.

The Romanesque Cathedral

Never before had there been an age in which the architecture was such a thoroughly unified composition in space, evenly perfected both inside and out. Egypt's temples were huge, hollowed-out blocks. Something

Plate 33. Hildesheim, St. Michael 1001-1033. View from the west.

similar can be seen in the buildings of the closely related culture of Babylon. In India proliferating shapes towered above each other without ever leading to a real experience of space. The Greek temple was one single space, but its interior had no architectural significance at all. Now, however, in the Romanesque cathedral, masses of space cluster together, and everything fits with everything else in a mutual and richly harmonious balance. On both sides the main area, or nave, is divided into different levels and accompanied by the aisles; its movement is powerfully interrupted by the transept, then carried forward in the choir but at the same time reversed in its direction there. Then there are the vertical masses of space in the spires: above the crossing, at the ends of the transept and on the western entrance side, unless there is a second choir at that point. Here, for the first time, something has come into being that deserves to be called a "building organism" (*Baukörper*): an organic structure with many parts that grows out into all dimensions of space (Plate 34).

Romanesque architecture has been called an "additive" style, in contrast to an "analytic" one. In an "additive" style a whole is formed through the accumulation of individual, independent structural and spatial elements, whereas in an "analytic" one the individual spatial elements come about when the whole, experienced as something original and primary, is subdivided. It is certainly the case to a large extent that Romanesque architecture is additive; in fact, this goes so far that—at least in its mature forms—the various large spaces of the interior seem to be made up of smaller, "partial" spaces, each of which has a certain self-contained independence from all the others. This is true, on the one hand, for the way the individual spaces fit together over each square of the floor plan formed by the position of the columns or pillars (especially in both the nave and the aisles of the longitudinal structure.) It is also true of the way the individual tiers—the arches or pillars below, the gallery, the triforium gallery, the clerestory windows—are set above each other. In the heights, the widths and the depths—wherever the roving eye looks it finds new spaces to see into.

It would be wrong, however, to understand "additive" in an outward sense, for its inner counterpart is a magnificent unity of the whole. Not a single part of this whole could be left out, and not one could be added. Each part lives in and on the deep relationship it has to every other one, supporting, completing and ennobling it. But there is more (Fig. 10).

The organization of the whole building derives from *one single element* which gives it the measure for its growth and the pulse-beat by which it lives. This is the *crossing* or square formed by the intersection of the nave and the transept. Applied to the rear of the building, it provides the proportions for the square of the choir; to the right and left, that of the transept itself; repeated three, four or five times toward the front, it delimits the nave; bisected, it is the measure for the aisles. It is the very heart of the medieval cathedral. At the moment of its "discovery," all the elements that had long been developing individually fell into place, and the Romanesque cathedral was born (Fig. 11).

The crossing had been around for a long time, and yet it had also not been around, for no one had ever really "seen" it before. Only now, in one of the great creative moments of human history, was its structural significance understood and its uniqueness emphasized by the arches

125

Plate 34. Maria Laach. Benedictine abbey on Lake Laach. 1093-1177.

above the square; at last it was really "there," and along with it, the cathedral as such.

The crossing arises at that point where transept and nave come together in a common area. In this area the movement of the one, flowing toward the choir, suddenly meets the transverse thrust of the other from the side and is momentarily held back, even though it is powerful enough to overcome this thrust and send out an arm for the choir on the other side. This "other side," which is the space for the altar and the people consecrated to its service, is in truth a world "beyond" of a completely different nature.

Now the force of this dammed-up movement, streaming backwards in all directions, creates the prototypal cell from out of which and whose measurements the whole colossal organism of the cathedral is born (or perhaps it is more accurate to say: reborn).

This was nothing less than a complete revolution, something unheard

Fig. 10. St. Michael's in Hildesheim. Reconstruction. Built between 1007 and 1033 under Bishop Bernward, who was later canonized. Remodelled several times in the following centuries, it was destroyed by bombs and fire in 1945. The reconstruction has attempted to restore the original building.

of until that moment: the formation and delimitation of an entire building out of a single element of space. Although not an outward center, the crossing becomes a center of gravity in an organic sense, the germ of an organism unfolding in space and the cell that both makes this organism grow and limits its growth.

All this happens from the inside. The whole body of the building is formed from this innermost core. Everything flows toward it, and out of it comes all of the force that models the building's form. The nave marches majestically toward it from far away; the choir presses in from the opposite side, as do the two arms of the transept from the right and left. Pushed upward by all this elemental energy, the tower rises above the crossing, bracing itself sturdily when heavy and massive and shooting upward when lighter and more slender—the elevation and revelation of that inner, mystery-filled world. On the other hand, the force striving upward in both it and its brother and sister towers on the western front is held in balance by the heavy, recumbent, horizontal masses of the building. A mysterious, flowing life streams through the entire work; it pours its activity into all dimensions of the space, surging up and down

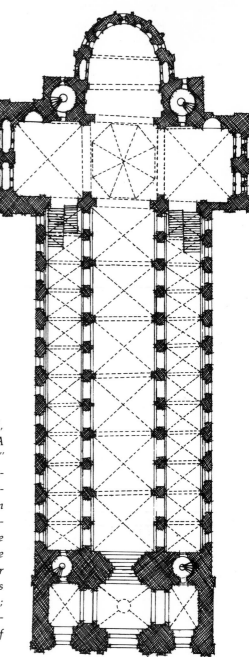

Fig. 11. Speyer, Cathedral, about 1040. Ground plan. A good example of the "system" which takes as the basic measurement for the whole structure the area of the intersection in which the nave and the transept cross. The bays of the nave, as well as those of the transept, are each erected over a square which is the same as the square of this intersection; the bays of the aisles are constructed over squares only half as long.

and back and forth, its powerful rhythm glorious and deeply satisfying. But again and again it returns to the crossing from where it started, like the blood to the heart.

This is the place to discuss in more detail the idea touched on earlier that the Germanic peoples are the ones who take up the Greek impulse again, keep it alive and bring it to a further stage of perfection. For in all the aspects of the Romanesque cathedral just described the ideals embodied in the Greek temples are still alive. They have merely undergone a significant metamorphosis. Proportion, organizational clarity, harmony of balance, overall comprehensibility and the well-balanced interplay of force are all more evident and more closely related to the archetype in the Romanesque cathedral than they are in the later buildings of the Renaissance, which breathe in an entirely different atmosphere.

In Greece this had all been said with an elemental simplicity appropriate to the initial statement of the theme. Now, in the Middle Ages, its culmination is rich and fulfilling. What was perceived earlier as the melody of Apollo, resounding from outside, has come all the way in. Now it is active from within, and fully mastered.

This is not meant in the sense of an external tradition, as though the architects of that era had studied Greek temples, for instance. Such a thing is simply out of the question. The process is much more inward and hidden, taking place in mysterious depths and at the same time far transcending man. The Greek temple, after all, was also only the "end of a path," the "expression" of a being whose innermost reality was to be found in the realm of the invisible. The wisdom of Paracelsus was also able to say of man, "We human beings are invisible people." What he means is that what we see of a human being is only the expression of something more real but invisible. In the same way, the Greek temple and Greek sculpture are only physical expressions of something greater and invisible that extends into human beings, becoming something in them and through them and thereby achieving a physical reality over long periods of time. What we mean here is that the Romanesque cathedral is an internalized "realization" of the very same being which first "expressed" itself through Greek art. The difference is that it reaches more deeply, working entirely from within, where it has undergone a significant metamorphosis.

The same being—and yet how changed! Not only does it express its complete entrance into physical matter by the way it shapes the masses

129

of space, whereas in Greece it was still only experienced at the borderline of the physical world; the most basic difference is that now, in the interior, gigantic spaces begin to arch overhead, and inner spaces open up. What spaces they are! The formative growth force that had come all the way into the basilica is now on full display and has sent out one space after another (Plate 35).

In such spaces the feeling of the space in the early Christian basilica is still very much alive. It is that "hyperspace," which in essence was not created for man at all. More self-contained—mainly because the mosaic is gone—and more composed, this space is something that still far transcends the human being. This impression is not due to external dimensions, even though it is strongest in the larger buildings, such as the eastern end of the cathedral in Strasbourg. In small chapels the effect is essentially just as intense. If we try to imagine who can actually "live in" these spaces and fill them out, we soon find ourselves thinking of beings of a higher order. Do they not really seem to be filled with the rustling of wings of gigantic angels?

There is also no position from which the whole inside can be seen or felt at once. New vistas are continually opening up from one of the partial spaces into another, but none is ever complete. From every vantage point—the aisle, the nave, the transept, the choir, the ambulatory or the choir gallery—one looks out of one space into another and is dimly aware of others. The closest spaces make a powerful impression, others seem somehow different, and the ones farthest away fade off into the distance.

And yet these spaces must have opened up somewhere within man himself. How else would he be able to represent them or settle into them and feel at home there? They have been taken hold of, after all, and something human must therefore contain them. Where do we look to find the larger wholeness that includes them within itself?

This question is the same as the question of how self-aware both architecture and man are at this time. It answers itself if we substitute for the word "additive" the word "collective," for we see then that man is building himself in the medieval cathedral as well.

For this is the age in which self-awareness is collective, although an individualizing principle produces many variations of this self-awareness.

Plate 35. Hildesheim, St. Michael's. Interior looking west.

It is also the age when knighthood and monastic communities determine the essential features of civilization. The self-awareness of the individual was his participation in the self-awareness of his group. What the group was depended on what the members of the group were; but what gave meaning to the individual's life and was the basis of his pride and feeling of worth was not whether he was this or that person, but whether he was a perfect member of his community or not, coming up to its standards in the fullest possible way.

That was also the structure of the Holy Roman Empire of the German Nation and the relationship which the emperor had to his princes. He was one of them, elected by them in their solemn assembly. He was dependent on their good will and strength. Their free association and cooperation formed the building or the body of the "empire." But he was also the one who gave order and form by setting standards and administering justice; everything oriented itself according to him, and his leadership was followed without question.

Yet even he did not gain his self-awareness out of himself. This was precluded by the fact that he often had to assume this office while still almost a boy. His consciousness grew out of what pervaded the whole empire. He did not find it "out of" himself, but he certainly did find it in himself. He was no pharaoh, boundlessly encompassing and permeating everything, nor was he the apex of a pyramid. But neither was "The Empire" a community like the Greek democracy, in which everyone jealously saw to it that no one rose above anyone else—a democracy to be borne equally by all as the temple was borne by its columns, each the same as all the others. A new principle was at work now, shaping both the single human being and the community and raising them up to a higher reality: individualizing and yet community-forming.

The Church was originally supposed to have been organized along similar lines, but the Roman lust for power, with its Egypt-like tendencies to unify everything, always falsified the originally pure picture.

The working of these communities made it possible for spaces to begin to open up in man. For these communities were determined from within and were formed to create space for something internal, not for some external purpose. Where the latter was nevertheless the case, as in

Plate 36. Strasbourg, Cathedral. Head of one of the "Virtues" from the right casing of the northwest portal. After 1276.

the ecclesiastical orders of knights, this external body was also subject to an inner factor, and well-considered rules kept the two in balance.

It was the age when men began to develop what we call "virtues." This was something new. The ideals of moderation, composure and level-headedness were already a part of Greek culture, of course, but the actual concept of "virtue" was still unknown, and the Roman *virtus* was something else again. The restraint inherent in just this concept was also unknown, as was virtue as an all-permeating and all-conquering force capable of transforming one's whole attitude toward life from within. Greece also did not yet know that natural forces could be held back and later overcome, molded and properly allocated by the force that was enhanced in this process and was used to create inner space. Nor did it know the other concept derived from this: *Werdekeit*, or dignity (Plates 36, 37, 38, 39).

> "Creator of all dignity
> Are you indeed, O Lady Moderation,
> And blessed is the man who has your teaching."
> (from the Middle High German)

Such were the impulses that nurtured the growth of those figures who were later portrayed so magnificently by Romanesque *sculpture* in its final and most mature stages as it was already tending toward the Gothic. (Until then, other elements, yet to be discussed, were more influential.) Chartres, Bamberg, Strasbourg, Freiburg and even Naumburg— how much these names call to mind! That age was well aware of its greatness. As Gottfried von Strasbourg wrote:

> "I shall never more surmise
> That in Mycenae sun doth rise;
> Perfect beauty ne'er dawned so clear
> In Greece's land, as it dawns here."
> (from the Middle High German)

What was dawning here was even more. The wondrous world of these sculptures, too, loudly proclaims that the God who had performed His glorious deeds from the outside in Greece is now working from with-

Plate 37. Strasbourg, Cathedral. The "Wise Virgins" from the southwest portal. After 1276.

in. How much comes to light in all these figures! What dignity! What tenderness and strength! What austerity and sweetness! What humility and self-assurance! What a wealth of *inner* form! How they feel the worth of what they bear within themselves, and how balanced and harmonious all these elements are each time they reunite in a new work of art! Inner spaces have opened here, indeed, spaces filled with flowing life, richly and deeply interwoven, which still hint at new, dim spaces in the distance.

And yet what dignity, clarity and relaxation their *outer* form displays at the same time: two worlds in a perfect state of balance.

This is the place to speak of something which is absolutely essential to the world of the Romanesque cathedral and which appears there as the balance between the principle of form and the principle of matter. For part of the joyous experience of the Romanesque cathedral is that the forces that shape it never quite overpower the massiveness of the walls— that elemental quality of the stone that lives in them and asserts itself with such power and deep satisfaction.

Here, from another direction, we come across the secret of balance as such. As one of the characteristic and fundamental secrets of the Romanesque style, it works throughout the cathedral as the balance between inner and outer structure, between ego-like and group-like, or vertical and horizontal forces. For this, after all, is clear: the Romanesque ends and the Gothic begins when the vertical, inner, ego-like forces or principle of form gain the upper hand over the horizontal, outer, group-like forces or principle of matter.

Now just what are these forces whose presence in the body of the walls is so powerful?

In the early works of the Romanesque period they are still completely hidden in the heavy masses of the walls. Silent at first, they very soon emerge. More and more the stone is loosened and broken up, and what is inside is lured out to the surface. This occurs first in the capitals and consoles, places which are already filled with this life in a special way because it collects there, and which are predestined to reveal it because a kind of meeting is taking place in them. But this opening up also occurs

Plate 38. Uta. Statue of one of the founders in the west choir of the cathedral in Naumburg. About 1250. These statues were not portraits of living persons. The representatives of the knightly society whose names they bear had already been dead for 200 years at the time they were portrayed.

where the inner world of the cathedral opens out into the outer world: in the soffits of the windows and on the portals, which become more and more impressive (Plate 40).

Everywhere figures and forms emerge from the walls. At first they are only flowing lines, intertwining ribbons, spirals, indentations and interlaced fillets; later on, fantastic plant forms, animal heads and animal members grow out of them. Finally, human forms emerge from these strange woven patterns.

It is correct, of course, to trace these phenomena back to the ancient Nordic and Celtic world of forms, and especially to the time of the great migrations of peoples. But the observation is only a preliminary one, and quite superficial, for the question immediately arises once again as to the reality and the nature of the experience behind this world of forms. This reality is *the experience of the elemental world.* This lively weaving and working and intertwining, this pressing forward and fleeing away again, this mysterious interwovenness is all a revelation of the same world the medieval alchemist experienced in his laboratory. Elemental beings suddenly show their faces and disappear again in a world filled with tremendous, creative dynamism.

This world is the one at work everywhere in the walls of the Romanesque cathedral. The figures which appear there have not been added on from the outside, but have all actually emerged from the massive stone of the walls, columns and pillars. Man, too, is born of this world and imbedded in the laws of its life. The figures standing there in the walls of the cathedrals—patriarchs and saints, kings and prophets, figures of a Holy Scripture which has been written not merely onto paper but into the whole of the earth—are all in the grip of that tremendous weaving. They themselves become a part of this mysterious forest. Totally imbedded in the order of this all-encompassing world, they do not emerge from it at any point or with a single one of their gestures. Their garments are woven from these forces in lines which merely act like folds (Plate 41).

In the souls of the people who created these works there must still have been something like a last, faint echo of the great and exalted world of the Druid mysteries and the Sacred Groves—a world where souls were immersed in the weaving of elemental forces, experienced, in turn, as the

Plate 39. Timo. Statue of a founder in the west choir of the cathedral in Naumburg. Cf. Plate 38.

reflection and lowermost manifestation of cosmic forces. Still alive in the souls of that time was a last, dreamy, clairvoyant vision of those worlds and a sensitivity to their activity, both in one's own body and in the world as a whole.

This alone is the world in which the Romanesque style was possible. The inner forces that could organize, conceive, understand and entice to the surface what had been inside had mastered this tremendous driving element—but had not yet overcome it. It was an infinitely fortunate moment in human history, and for this reason alone man was able to make a home for himself in those immense spaces, filled as they were with cosmic life. For this reason alone could he surround them and include them in his own being. It was a world he could still encompass with his understanding. In these buildings something still lives of the infinitely pure spirituality of the Scotch-Irish monks who were the first to bring the message of the Son of God, who had come into the world and risen from the dead, to large parts of France and Germany. They proclaimed Him as the "Lord of the Elements." He, the Lord of the Elements, is the one who with power and with silence moves through these spaces—and through the human spaces of medieval man—and lives in them. Throughout this whole epoch, Christ continues to be experienced in His cosmic character. The rainbow is still just high enough to be His throne, and He reaches up into the world of stars.

But He has entered the earth, the human space, and ever and again He rises there in the miracle of the sacrament, out of the earthly elements of the bread and wine, from within. For it is His nature to be "from within."

What else does the Romanesque cathedral proclaim than that the Lord of the Sun has become "the Lord of the Elements," and that the being whom Greece had worshipped in the apollonian power of the sun has entered the earthly world, penetrating it and leading it to rebirth? That is the feeling for the world which found immediate expression, or "manifestation," in Romanesque art. These buildings proclaim that mighty cosmic process of Christ's entrance into the earthly world, the impregnation of the earth with the power of the sun.

Then, however, a moment comes when He can no longer be found even within this sphere of the world.

Plate 40. Murrhardt, Chapel of Walderich. Round arch window of the choir. 1220-1230.

141

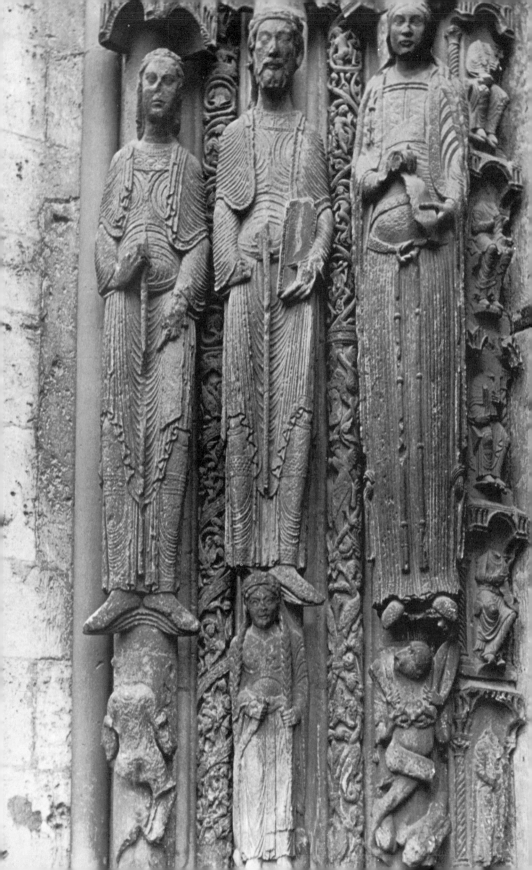

This wondrous world of the Romanesque cathedral was a last bright glow of those forces in their decline. For just those other forces, whose desire it was to comprehend, now had to push this world aside as they grew stronger and stronger (in the same way as in the fairy tale, where the curiosity of a human being who wants to understand drives away the friendly elemental beings). When this moment had arrived, the Romanesque style became the Gothic.

The Birth of the Gothic

The century from 1150 to 1250 is the period of the most beautiful and most mature flowering of the Romanesque style in Germany, while at the same time the new world of the Gothic is dawning in France. This century also witnesses the high point of medieval civilization and is the time when everything great which we owe to this civilization originates. What a gathering of noble spirits! *Parzival, Titurel* and *Lohengrin* were written then, as well as the *Song of the Nibelungen*. It is the golden age of minnesong and of the troubadours. Wolfram von Eschenbach, Walther von der Vogelweide, Chrétien de Troyes, Thomas Aquinas, Albertus Magnus, St. Elisabeth and St. Francis of Assisi were all living at that time. To describe this century in detail and do justice to its inner meaning would require a whole work by itself.

This remarkable century is one of the most important border areas in the spiritual life of mankind as a whole. The transition from the Romanesque to the Gothic is by no means caused merely by the discovery of the pointed arch and the ribbed vault. It is the "expression" of the transition from one feeling for the world to another, and the point where the new world divides off from the old can be located quite exactly, as the root from which everything else has sprung.

This is an event which in modern history books is only treated in passing: the dispute between the *Nominalists* and the *Realists*. This

Plate 41. Chartres. Kings and Queens in the casing of the left side-portal of the west front. About 1150.

143

dispute was more than a simple squabbling among philosophers. For the Realists declared that concepts are present *ante rem*, i.e., before the individual phenomena of the world of the senses, and are therefore "real." The Nominalists, on the other hand, declared them to be *post rem*, i.e., only subsequently abstracted from the phenomena by the human intellect, and therefore mere *nomina*, or names. The Realists leaned on Plato's doctrine of ideas for their support, whereas the Nominalists established the position of Aristotle's abstractions which was to dominate all the following centuries until the age of Humanism. What this means is that in the Realists, a way of thinking was defeated for which the world of ideas was still something objective; in the Nominalists, a way of thinking assumed prominence which could no longer have this experience, since for it thoughts were no longer divine revelations but mere products of the human mind.

Anselm of Canterbury maintained, *credo, ut intelligam*, and Abelard countered with, *intelligo, ut credam*.[11] But the two were speaking at cross purposes, because to each one of them both the *credo* and the *intelligo* meant something different. It was still Anselm's experience that through the power of faith he could raise himself into that sphere where the divine, creative, cosmic thoughts have their home. Abelard had to say that the spiritual world was closed, and that in order to draw near to it he was forced to develop and apply his own human intelligence.

We must try to feel the whole tragic grandeur of what was taking place. The fact that the Nominalists won out was the death sentence for the entire world over which the Romanesque cathedral had spanned its arches. But it also meant that from that point on man was turned out into a loneliness which, until then, had been inconceivable. Before this time there had still been echoes of the Greek experience of being in touch with the gods at least in the world of thought. Now, even that had ceased.

Such was the process which set this whole great century in movement. In some places it went on more rapidly than in others, but it never failed to occur. Characteristically, it began in France. This is why the Gothic originated there, while in Germany, more than 100 years later, works continued to appear in which there was still an afterglow of the world which farther to the West had long since vanished.

One explanation for this really quite strange phenomenon has been that this was the time of the great Hohenstaufen emperors, in which Germany was so powerful and proud of its strength that it had no need to look beyond its borders. Actually, just the opposite is the case. The

French Gothic was known in Germany. In fact, as is generally known, many individual features were taken over from French buildings. The truth is that under the Hohenstaufens the German imperial majesty was able to shine out once more in such magnificence because the Romanesque was still alive in Germany. Stated more precisely, it was because the forces which find expression in the Romanesque style continued to be active and by that time had become so free that they could reveal themselves in all their glory. It was a matter of destiny that the old, naturelike forces bound up with the elemental world were stronger in Germany than they were in France, which was a product of a much more variegated mixture of races. It has already been shown how the nature of the medieval empire was related to the nature of the Romanesque cathedral. It was *one* great world. By 1254, when the last of the Hohenstaufen princes sank so tragically into his grave, taking with him the idea of the Empire—for what followed the interregnum was the same as what had been there before in name only—, these forces were exhausted in Germany, too, and the Gothic had moved in victoriously on every hand. With the death of Konrad IV a whole world sank into its grave. That was the end of the world which Joachim de Floris had foretold, confusing inner and outer reality in typical medieval fashion. The process which had begun with the dispute between the Realists and the Nominalists was now complete.

Another event of these times became an especially vivid pictorial expression of this process.

In the 12th century a far-reaching *transformation of the altar* had taken place. Until that time the canopied altar had been in general use. Now it was replaced by the retable altar, i.e., one with a rear wall, or reredos. The priest, who had formerly stood on the back side of the altar facing the congregation when he celebrated the mass, now moved around to their side of it and stood with his back to them, facing the altar just as they did. At the same time the cross came to occupy its fixed position on the altar, and the large groups of crucifixes on the rood loft came into existence, as well as the liturgical crucifixes on the triumphal arches.

The importance of this transformation is that from now on the "world here" and the "world beyond" are separated once and for all. Until that time it had been possible—for a single person, at least, if not any longer for the congregation—to stand "on the other side." The "beyond" was still within man's reach. Now, this too is at an end.

At the same time the importance of the cross was increasing as an expression of how deeply men were affected by the world of death. The spiritual world was closed off, and all efforts of mankind were directed solely toward breaking through into its light and into its life again. People sought to do this in two different ways: one was the outer path, the way of scholasticism; the other was the inner path, the way of mysticism. The Gothic encompasses them both. And if Gothic cathedrals have been spoken of as "heaven-storming," there is more truth to this than is generally supposed. The Gothic cathedrals want to take heaven by storm —the heaven that has been lost, but is now within them. The fervor of the will to do this is deeply moving.

We do not need to add much more, since the essential groundwork for the understanding of this world has now been laid and needs only a little amplification here and there. The absolute withdrawal of the Gothic into itself has already been made clear. All that is important now is the inner space, and the only places where the cathedral's outer structure is taken hold of by forces that shape it are the ones where this inner world opens itself to the outside. These are the portals and the west wall, which by now has become the "front wall" and is definitively marked as the entrance side, a development intimately bound up with the transformation of the altar. All other elements have had to accept the fact that the supporting structure of the flying buttresses and outer pillars demotes them to being the back side of the interior surface (Plates 42/43).

The formative forces that subdivide and organize have now gained the upper hand, and they end by absorbing everything in the way of elemental substance that was in the heavy Romanesque walls. What lives in these buildings is a fervent yearning to completely dissolve the walls and to strip them of all matter so that as little wall as possible is left. Some choirs and even whole churches have collapsed because the builders were far too bold in their elimination of the supporting walls. What was left in the pillars and the ribs of the vaults was only enough to be called something like "lines of force." For in essence, the pillars, ribs, columns and shafts contain only the smallest possible amount of material needed to fill out an abstract structural dynamic. The material substance has been "thought to pieces."

Plate 42. Freiburg i. Br. Cathedral. The transept is still Romanesque. The nave and especially the western spire, which is praised again and again for its singular beauty, are pure Gothic. About 1275 to about 1350.

146

The same passion is alive in this that expressed itself in scholasticism as the passionate desire to understand: the longing to understand the miracle of the divine. No one is able to perceive its reality directly any longer, contain this reality within himself or build himself into its spaces. And so, dogma arises; its essential features have been worked out earlier, of course, but only now does it develop the full force of its coercive power. This is how the Inquisition and the persecutions of the heretics came about, fueled basically by a great and terrible fear that when even dogma no longer holds, everything must fall apart, and the great unity of the world will collapse completely.

The vertical forces have gained the upper hand over the horizontal ones. This interior is a single, passionate upward drive that sweeps everything along with it. The entire space is so filled with this upward-shooting movement that there is no way to come to a real feeling of space. The cathedrals grow taller and taller, and their powerful upward thrust becomes more and more uncompromising in its exclusion of every horizontal element that would suggest rest.

A comparison with the Greek temple is most informative at this point. Both are "static" styles. But the life of the Greek temple is in the wonderful *equilibrium* between its load-bearing forces and its forces of weight; the Gothic cathedral draws its life from the way it fervently *overcomes* weight. The upward-striving force in its columns grows and grows until it eats its way into the heavy beams, shatters their horizontality and turns them upright to form pointed arches.

Overcoming is the word that best characterizes the Gothic. The fervor that struggles in the columns to overcome weight is the same as the one in the walls that wants to forcibly overcome matter—the body in which man is imprisoned—and to loosen and break up everything that has become dense and dark. It is this boundless longing for the light that leaves nothing of the walls but windows. Windows to where? What stood in these windows in glowing colors were the saints. They were windows into the beyond (Plate 43).

It is the same fervor which makes the flagellants lacerate their bodies. Never did mankind experience the "fall" of man as strongly as it did then,

Plate 43. Cologne. Interior of the cathedral. Design by Master Gerhard in 1248. Consecration of the choir in 1322. After that, the building activity stopped and was only taken up again and completed from 1842 to 1880.

the fall into heaviness, matter, darkness and death, the exclusion from paradise. This whole age is one single assault on the barred and bolted gates of paradise and the formidable angel with his flaming sword. But that is an assault on being born. Pinder once said about the choir of Beauvais, "Here men wanted to learn to fly." Indeed they did, but like weightless, blessed spirits. The boundless longing of the Gothic cathedrals for light had nothing to do with external light. In these windows dwells a light that has become a part of the element of life, broken up in a magical interplay of unbelievably glowing colors. What matters here is the "beyond." It is a matter of breaking through into the inner light, the light of the spiritual world, of overcoming all death and even forcing the very stone to blossom and seem to have a fragrance. Towers, too, grow and grow, becoming lighter and more full of light as they rise from storey to storey until at their very peak, now but a distillate of everything earthly, they culminate in the finial and blossom toward heaven—ready to shatter, if only this earth will then be "overcome."

> "For love I'd gladly die, could that but be my plight,
> For that one I did spy, with my eyes full of light,
> A-standing in my soul, whom I do love aright."

This is mysticism, born of the Gothic spirit.

Scholasticism, on the one hand, develops a passion for working out subtler and subtler definitions to the point where its excesses seem so ridiculous and incomprehensible to us today. On the other hand, mysticism is only just beginning to develop its deep and fervent meditations on the suffering and death of Christ and eventually arrives at forms which strike us today as tasteless and even repulsive. But all these things are only metamorphoses of the same fundamental desire: to storm the bolted gates of heaven.

The same fervor glows in Gothic *sculpture* so that the body is twisted under its pressure and consumed to the point of an almost transparent fragility. The garments swell, crumple and rustle in this restive yearning for God (Plate 44).

Plate 44. Rottweil, Lorenz Chapel. Wooden sculpture of St. Gallus of Schörzingen from about 1480.

Gothic and Islam

We do not understand the full significance of the Gothic, however, until we view it against the background of the other great culture which blossomed so magnificently at the same time in its own way, the *culture of Islam*. If the emergence of heretics represented a threat to the waning Middle Ages because of their tendency toward individualization, Islam was perhaps an even greater threat because it denied the impulse toward individualization altogether.

There are related elements in both cultures, and the two cultures have actually influenced each other to a certain extent. But in the final analysis what they display is a cultural polarity of significance for the whole history of the world. Even when they use the same words, they mean something completely different by them.

One of the things which some people believe the West took over from Islam is also one of the characteristic features of the Gothic style, namely, the pointed arch. This very feature, however, is one that can be used to make the whole difference between the two cultures absolutely clear.

In its pure form the pointed arch is rarely found in Islamic architecture. Wherever it occurs, it has either been pressed down to an obtuse angle or has largely absorbed the verticals into itself. In both cases the experience it gives rise to is very different from that of the Gothic pointed arch. More frequently it merges with the horseshoe arch or takes on the form of the keel arch. The gesture of these arches becomes quite clear when they appear in the form of a cupola, with the strange onion shape which is so characteristic of it (Plate 45). What does this shape express?

Nothing less than the same experience on which the Gothic is based, the experience of being closed off. But it expresses this with the opposite sign, so to speak; the Gothic arch is a most fervent expression of that longing to overcome, whereas the Islamic one is an intense expression of affirmation or densification and of the finality of being closed off by being born.

But the contrasts are even more extensive. Christian architecture created spatial shapes everywhere, groups of enormous vaulted spaces. The Islamic will to build asserts itself from the very beginning in the creation of single spaces; it is also inclined to make the shape of the space illu-

Plate 45. Isfahan. Main liwan of the madrasa Chahar-Bagh. Built by Shah Hussein from 1706 to 1714.

sory by a veritable forest of pillars and columns (Plate 46). In its great domed structures, however, it achieves this by dissolving the surfaces into a playful arabesque of light and shadows.

In western art the will to form interior spaces that have a life from within themselves undergoes a glorious revival—individualizing, but also breathing and emanating an awareness of its own worth and dignity. Wherever this happens in western art, we find everywhere in Islam the spacelessness of the surface and the unifying abstract line. This line is in motion, but is not moving toward any goal or showing any will to overcome. It is only getting lost in its own purposeless meandering. It does not form images; it only dissolves them. The Islamic hostility toward images has a much deeper foundation than a mere decree of the Koran.

Both the Gothic and the Islamic worlds are expressions of the new forces of intelligence that become increasingly stronger as they approach. But how differently these forces are applied! The Christian West directs them solely toward the goal of understanding the miracle of God's becoming man and of His ever new incarnation in the sacrament. These forces turn inward as servants and co-workers in man's fervent longing to take heaven by storm. In this way the Christian West comes to develop the mighty structure of scholasticism, a philosophy that exists to serve theology. Its concern is not to understand the outer world, but only the divine one, which is still effective through the medium of faith, even though it is no longer visible.

The outer world, however, is just the one toward which Islam directs its efforts, creating an imposing natural science, a system of medicine, mathematics, astronomy, and in a certain sense even a technology. It develops all those sciences and forces of abstraction under which the earth rigidifies in lifeless uniformity and senselessness. It knows only this earthly life, a life without miracles and without gods, and its heaven, its "beyond," is only a more enjoyable version of life on earth.

The cathedral of the West—the house it builds—is both a shelter for the altar and a reverential "comprehension" of the miracle that the divine rises like the sun in the midst of mankind itself and that an infinite heaven will go forth from the very earth.

The mosque of Islam—the house that it builds—does not have an altar. The devotion of the believers is not concentrated on any specific place within their midst but on one outside them and far away—the

Plate 46. Cordoba. Omayad Mosque. 785-990. 19 aisles with 620 columns.

154

Kaaba in Mecca. This, however, is not a place where the earthly opens to reveal the infinite radiance of heaven. It is a stone—one that fell from heaven, but now only stone and nothing else.

Islam was unique in the way it developed the very forces through which the earth becomes a grave. And the sacred stone it worships—the Kaaba in Mecca or the rock in Jerusalem—is in reality, though not outwardly, of course, the stone on the tomb of the Redeemer.

This is why in those times the call to "free the tomb from the hands of the infidels" found such a resonant echo in the hearts of western Christendom, who followed it by the thousands and tens of thousands, leaving everything behind them. This is true even for the times when this sacred desire became contaminated with all sorts of other desires that were not so sacred, and when it was occasionally misused for entirely different purposes. Much more was at stake than a little patch of earth that sheltered a cherished memory. Deep down, these souls must have been aware of this. What was at stake was the destiny of the entire earth, the destiny of man.

For what mankind was going through at that time was something like a second entombment of Christ. The age of the Romanesque cathedrals had still experienced Him in the elemental realm of the earth. Now He was no longer to be found. He was hidden in the earth. The West, however, knew that the earth conceals within it the power of the resurrection and of heaven and that the stone had been rolled away. It knew this seed of the divine and fervently believed in it. It could not allow the stone to be rolled over the tomb again so that the second, greater resurrection would be prevented. People were ready to sacrifice everything they had and go to their deaths, ready to be broken to pieces and to endure the most severe tortures so that this sun might rise.

Whether they went toward the east, or westward to those parts of Spain that had been conquered by the Arabs, the crusades were only the most "outward" expression of a spiritual struggle that was not really decided on the battlefields of Palestine but in the souls of western humanity and was fraught with conclusions of far-reaching significance.

This struggle reached its climax in the conflict between Thomas Aquinas and Averroes. Averroes had taught that after death the human soul dissolves away into a universal spirituality. Over against this, Thomas had successfully defended the immortality of the individual human being. The whole world took a passionate interest in this struggle and was deeply justified in doing so, for the matter was much more than

156

a question for specialists in philosophy. What was at stake was the very essence of man, the question of whether the human being is formed and determined from out of an eternal, indestructible core—from within outwards—or solely from outside, having originated solely through the coming together of certain elements of the outer world.

The situation was similar to the one at the time of the Persian Wars. Both times it was "Man" that was at stake. But at that time it was the dull, animal-like forces of the Orient that were attempting to overpower him. Now it is the forces of the intellect that threaten him with a stultifying rigidification. If Arabism had won out, the direct consequence would have been a proliferation of materialism and the destruction of human individuality on an inconceivable scale. No "Faust" would ever have been written, nor would the music of Beethoven and Bruckner ever have resounded. In the following centuries a purely intellectual way of viewing the world grew rampant, although it was somewhat subdued. If such a view had become firmly established already at that time, the whole culture of the West would have been in question, for materialism, which reduced man to the level of the highest animal and degraded the world to a conglomeration of indifferent physical and chemical processes, was nothing but a continuation of Arabism. This is a point often emphasized by Rudolf Steiner.

At the time of the Persian Wars, the places where the most decisive battles were fought were the construction sites of the temples, the workshops of the sculptors and the halls of the philosophers; now, they are the construction sites of the churches and cathedrals and the cells of the scholars.

For the task at hand was to conjure up the reality of inner space, the reality of overcoming all heaviness, the reality of unity in diversity and the reality of the miracle in our midst. Such is the fervor of these buildings, which moves us so deeply even today, and their significance in world history as well.

Mystery

Everything described so far is actually only foreground. The energies, experiences and feelings of human beings are only the river bed in which a greater event is carving out a path for itself. This only becomes clear

157

when we once again look back over the whole development from the early Christian basilica to the great Gothic churches and cathedrals. What we see in it is the steady, living advance of the process that had first made itself known in the triumphal arch and the basilica: the fact that the God had entered.

For the being that creates its body for itself in the early Christian basilica and in the architecture of the Romanesque and Gothic churches is one and the same, just as it is the same being which lives in the seed, unfolds in the leaves, and blossoms in the flower. These are merely phases of an evolutionary process, metamorphosing from one to the next in different spheres and revealing themselves with an ever-increasing intensity.

By turning the structure of the Greek temple "inside out," the early Christian basilica had proclaimed that the God whose creative power had been experienced until then in the surrounding world had now come inside. The mosaics also spoke of this as they tried in their own way to make visible the nonspatial, divine world glowing with a superearthly light as it broke through the walls and entered from the outside. In Romanesque architecture it became apparent how this God creates spaces from the inside in the process of taking on a body. Growing out of the breath of its inner spaces, the "building organism" sends out extension after extension of itself in all directions. What happens in the Gothic as a continuation of this process?

The splendid and overwhelming development of these buildings was actually the result of a contraction. Once, their many parts and spaces had all been on a more or less equal footing; then they became the servants of one single element which outgrew them all and partially absorbed them into itself: the nave. The aisles are now only something like ambulatories, or "shells of space" (Jantzen), around this central core. The galleries have disappeared entirely. This development made it possible for the wall of the nave to develop the great walls of windows in its uppermost part. Now, however, it seems that all the forces of the nave wall itself are concentrated in the upward-striving columns and shafts. The same thing can be observed in the spires. In the Romanesque era, one storey had simply been set on top of another. Now, a single force becomes visible and palpable in its mighty upward growth as it penetrates right through every detail of the structure.

This force, emerging so powerfully on every side, is none other than the one we saw stretching up in the Egyptian obelisk in front of the entrance to the temple as a symbol of the sun. The difference is that now it has come all the way inside, where it permeates the entire "body" of the building, overcoming the heaviness of everything earthly, dissolving all the darkness of the matter away into light and transforming all materiality into pure form. This is the force which, first of all, has transformed the aisles. For the lower arcades of the nave are what now forms the actual boundary of its space, and the aisles themselves, reaching deep into space, are only the first and lowest phase of a process in which the outer wall, conceived of now as an enormous mass, will be hollowed out and dissolved. The character of the "diaphanous" wall which becomes more and more transparent could not be expressed more directly than it is in the area of the triforium gallery located directly above this. Here, the heaviness of the mass has been overcome to such a degree that the outer wall, broken up towards the interior by the arcades of the triforium gallery, is like a prelude to the triumph which then finally breaks out in such indescribable glory in the colorfully glowing windows. Everything of a spatial and material nature has been overcome. The earthly is shining outward from within.

The God who has entered and taken on a body, and who takes on a body again and again, has taken hold of this body from within. What has begun to glow is the mystery of transformation and transubstantiation.

It is not surprising that in the classical century of the Gothic the thinking of the dogmatists never ceases to revolve around the central mystery of transubstantiation, as does that of the liturgists around the Elevation, or the raising of the Host. Nor is it surprising that this is the very century in which the great epic poems begin to be written that deal with the Holy Grail. Everywhere the same secret is stirring in the depths of human souls, seeking to express itself in every sphere.

We are now in a position to understand the apocalyptic nature of Christian church architecture. When a church was built, it was always made of bodily substance which had been transformed and renewed from within, and this substance came not only from man but from the entire earth. In the churches and cathedrals people were really building away at the "heavenly Jerusalem," and were actually quite aware of this. Its turrets and pinnacles are the ones visible in the canopies above the saints. Today we know that this was already the idea and attitude behind the early basilicas. We must just be careful not to forget that people built what they experienced and tried to make visible what they actually felt, namely, that a transforming force had entered which was creating a future and a new body for the earth.[12]

The figure that makes the strongest impression on us, however, as it wanders on its way through the Middle Ages is that of the Virgin and the Child. She, more than anything else, is the object of medieval man's fervent love. The reason for this is that in this figure the deepest secret of the age has become an image which is born from its heart and so can speak to the heart in such a direct and moving way.

This image is not only the sign of something remembered; it is an intensely immediate experience. It is both history and myth—the representation of a reality which is a direct experience, but history only insofar as this direct experience within the realm of humanity is the consequence of a historical event. She is a representation, a pictorial evaluation; the "expression" of the human which by some miracle contains within it an element of the divine, and the "expression" of the earthly which has been lifted up, to the end that it may become the mother of something superearthly.

This, then, is the meaning of the Middle Ages for the world as a whole, as it came to be expressed in their dramas and their poetry, the crusades and the social order, in scholasticism and mysticism, and in the whole marvelously overarching structure: the fact that, in holy awe of the miracle in their midst, they "carried" this divine sun-being whom the world had received into itself in the mighty earthquake at the turning point of time and gave Him the space to work His way deeper and deeper into the realm of the earth.

All the churches and cathedrals, even when they do not bear her name, are songs of praise to "Notre Dame," "Our Lady." Like a song of triumph, one representation of the Virgin and the Child appeared by the thousands after Thomas's victory, thereby showing what great interest there had been in this struggle and its outcome. She is shown standing on the crescent moon, in which the dark countenance of the Arabic scholar, Averroes, is visible: Saved is the birth of the divine within the earth. The future of the earth is safe (Plate 47).

Plate 47. Mary and Child on the Crescent Moon. Ulm, Museum. Ascribed to Hans Multscher (1410-1467). Supposedly from Bihlafingen near Ulm.

VII

THE SUNRISE

Art at the Dawn of the New Age

A remark by Ulrich von Hutten expresses, as do few others, the mood and the character of the centuries in which our age began: "It is a joy to be alive . . ." But it only sounds the way it should when we hear it against the background of the great and terrible "Miserere" that resounded throughout the waning Middle Ages: the cries and sighs of the flagellants winding through villages and cities, the mournful songs of thousands of penitents, the fervent prayers echoing through cathedrals, the fear and uncertainty about the salvation of the soul which led to the crackling fires of the cruel stakes of the Inquisition, the thousandfold curses of life. Suddenly someone goes riding through the world, crying, "*iuvat vivere . . .*," and from all sides his cry comes echoing back a thousandfold: from the noisy workshops of metal-casters, wood-carvers and sculptors, the quieter ones of painters, the hidden rooms of scholars, the splendor of princely courts, the festive palaces of the aristocracy, the hustle and bustle in the vaults of merchants, the ships on the seas of the world, the songs of the itinerant scholars on their way from one school to the next, the faces of proud and mighty leaders of mercenary armies: "A joy to be alive . . .!"

A new world day is dawning with all its might. Something like the groaning of great iron gates being opened or the thundering song of a morning that will last for thousands of years runs through all its life and activity—and even through its suffering. There had only been a movement of such magnitude and significance some 2000 years earlier, when the genius of Greece emerged, and again 2000 years before that, when the mighty gods of Egypt began their rule. The change in human souls is tremendous as man enters a new kind of worldly space.

The forces of this new world begin to stir already toward the end of the 14th century. They wake up everywhere, assuming a variety of forms in Italy, France and Germany. The process of forming new nations, each with its own characteristic traits, had begun during the transition from the Romanesque to the Gothic; by now this process is complete. But whatever appears as something new, in one form here and another there, is only a metamorphosis of the one great force underlying it all which presses onward to the light with an elemental power.

Once we have seen this, we will be able to recognize the full extent of this movement. But to see it we will need to find broader concepts and ideas than the ones generally associated with the concept of the "Renaissance," for the Renaissance in Italy is only a partial and special manifestation of a much larger occurrence, and even its development in Germany gives a picture of its significance that is almost clearer and more impressive.

Now that this has been said, we may—or must—say the following as well. In what appears during these centuries something else is born that has been growing for a long time. The hidden, "prenatal" life and maturation of the new being can be followed clearly enough, and it is one of the most wonderful and fascinating processes which one can have the privilege of observing. For the character of the whole Christian Middle Ages from the Romanesque on, and especially during the Gothic, is strongly determined by two major factors: on the one hand, by the way an old world comes to an end, gradually at first, but more and more rapidly as time goes by, with an increasing sense of awareness; and on the other, by the quiet, mysterious, "subterranean" growth of a seed for which this age was a true and faithful womb, unknowingly full of wisdom.

One consequence of this fact, however, is that the transition to the new age occurs almost imperceptibly at first. The Middle Ages continue to work on from the past, and people often believe they are still in them, only to find all of a sudden that they are standing in the midst of a whole new world. For what is customarily called "late Gothic" is fundamentally already an expression of the fact that a new world has come to maturity.

Architecture

Both the Romanesque and the Gothic cathedral had preserved the basic form of the basilica: the nave, a leader among its companions, towered above the aisles, but their forces were the ones that bore it upward. The main space was in the center, accompanied by the more quietly dreaming spaces at its sides. In this way the cathedral became more and more intense as it tried to grow beyond itself, filled with a surging and a flooding of tremendous movement and of forces that never subsided as they nourished each other's growth.

In Germany, however, a development had already set in with the beginning of the Gothic which was destined to preserve the individual forms of the Gothic and yet dissolve them from the inside and alter their fundamental character. The aisles had grown upward until they were the same height as the nave. In the process, the clerestory windows, which until then had towered above the side spaces, had receded to the outer walls of these spaces, and a single, steep roof now covered the large inner space of the *hall church* (Plate 48).

This was the first sign of a development of far-reaching significance. The dynamics involved in the relationships of high and low, wide and narrow or dark and light spaces to one another receded in favor of a great unification of the space. The breathtaking movement of the basilica form gave way to a greater and greater sense of "space at rest."

In the 14th century this form of building spreads across the whole of Germany, and in the 15th century it becomes the standard principle of construction. At the same time, a fundamental transformation of all parts of the building begins, as an indication of how completely what lives in this form of architecture has been taken hold of.

The first element to be transformed is the vaulted ceiling. The Gothic cathedral had driven it upward to greater and greater heights as one aspect of its effort to dissolve it completely in striving for dematerialization. That was something that already lay in the nature of the ribbed vault. Not being an actual solid ceiling, but charged with movement all the way to the keystone of the vault in its ribs, where all its force is concentrated, it would like to let heaven shine through and reach right up into heaven itself. It is not really an end in itself, but points beyond itself into another world and is at most an image of that world in which all upward-striving forces finally come to rest.

Plate 48. Dinkelsbühl, St. George. Interior. Built from 1448 to 1499 by Nikolaus Eseler, father and son. Hall church with fan vaulting and ambulatory.

Now, however, vault forms appear which outwardly still seem Gothic but in actuality exude a very different atmosphere. These are the *"decorated" vaults* (as in the cathedral in Erfurt, the Liebfrauenkirche in Halle a.d.S., St. Anna in Annaberg i.S., St. Georg in Dinkelsbühl and many others). More and more ribs are added to the four or six customarily present, thereby subdividing the surfaces of the vaults into smaller and smaller segments and creating an intricate and often quite charming network. But these ribs have no function; they are nothing but ornament and decoration, and the moment this happens their effect becomes just the opposite. Instead of dissolving, they seem to become denser. Of course, their inherent movement does not come to a stop right away. At first these vaults are like waves surging excitedly in a storm; no longer so airy, they are more like a heavy liquid. But the densification process continues, until in the end the vaults are every bit as heavy and solid as the Italian coffered ceilings.

For the other thing going on up there is that the ceiling is becoming a unified surface. In the Gothic cathedral each individual part of the space still had a quiet, self-contained vault all to itself. This was true not only for the larger sections, such as the nave and the aisles, but for each separate square and rectangular bay as well. In the decoration, however, these boundaries dissolve, and the individual vaults all merge to form a single, tight structure. *One* ceiling spans *one* space.

This change has also led to a fundamental change in the nature of the pillars, or *piers*, for their character was intimately interwoven with the previous form of the vault.

The Gothic clustered pier consisted solely of "shafts," or engaged columns. It was a collection of functions, or "lines of force," and was filled with a single, upward-streaming inner life of infinite intensity. Only when it met its neighboring piers in the transverse arches, the wall arches or the diagonal arches did this movement come to rest. But this meeting was essentially always one which only took place in the infinite, in the beyond. The pier itself was not a mainstay and a support, for by drawing the shafts downward it had taken the whole burden into itself, which it did not then just "carry," but "overcame."

Besides the heaviness of the roof it had also taken in the density of the wall. To the extent that it had done so, it was still able to determine the form of the space. For even though the actual wall between the piers had disappeared by being absorbed into their movement, the boundary of the

166

space remained, invisibly stretched out from one pillar to the next. All that was missing was the material substance tht had formerly filled out the space. The Gothic cathedral, too, was woven together out of nothing but partial spaces, although this was less emphasized than it was in the Romanesque. In the early hall churches it was even less noticeable, but still perceptible. The piers formed boundaries for these spaces and closed them off, at least insofar as they did not actually negate the space itself by sweeping it upwards and evaporating it.

Under the broad, unified ceiling of the decorated vaults the shafts have lost their meaning. They are powerless to absorb this ceiling, and it would make no sense to absorb it anyway. They either fall away entirely or stay on in the form of graceful decoration. To compensate for this, however, the physical core of the pier emerges, which until now has been invisible and often not even actually present in a material sense. The pier becomes a column, a mainstay and support on which the roof rests.

But now there is a flood of space around it. The pier no longer stands at the edge of the space. Suddenly it stands in the middle, surrounded by the flow of space. Only when it reaches the outside walls does this freely breathing space find its boundaries, self-contained and at rest within itself. The tremendous sweeping movement is at an end. What emerges from it in all its grandeur and freedom is the event of *inner space*. It is no longer the relationship of one space to another, but *space itself*.

Once more the secret of the Middle Ages—their archetypal phenomenon—comes into focus. The Middle Ages were continuously confronted by the mystery of inner space and in fact even stood within it. However, by constantly stringing partial spaces together, they created interior spaces which in the end were essentially experienced from outside. Standing in any one of them, one would experience the adjoining ones much more strongly. Any given partial space was much too steep and narrow to become a real experience. Passing from one of the partial spaces into the others, one could sense how the new ones would recede when they were entered. The interior space was present everywhere, but it resisted all attempts to enter it. Its secret—the being of man—hovered over all Christian art from its very beginning. But it still stayed in the background, as if concealed. That was the character of the Middle Ages.

The archetypal phenomenon of the age now dawning reveals itself in the fact that man *enters* the interior space. At the same time, what he is entering is a new cosmic space; for this step can only be regarded as a cosmic event, since he now enters the space of worlds which has been his goal for thousands of years. This is a process of immeasurable magnitude, and its revolutionary consequences are very far-reaching. We who live half a millenium later are still in its midst.

Man enters interior space. This does not mean that the late Gothic hall church was already a perfect example of "interior space." In a process of such significance, a statement like this would be out of the question. The hall church is only a first transitional form, in which the entrance of the new forces is clearly delineated solely in what has been handed down through the architectural tradition. It will take several centuries yet before solutions to this new problem are really derived entirely from the substance of the new world. The process is similar to the way in which a human being incarnates. The young child is still largely determined by the environment he is born into, right into the physical substance which he receives from his parents. Nevertheless, his own, new being delineates itself very clearly in him, and later on it will create its own foundation entirely out of itself and slowly reverse the whole relationship by reaching out creatively into its environment, including the "environment" of its own body, giving it shape and direction.

At any rate, the motif that has been sounded in the hall church is pure, strong and unforgettable. The physicality of this church is the "expression" of a new kind of man. The people who have built this space are no longer filled solely with the urge to grow beyond themselves, overcome themselves or allow themselves to be overcome by some overwhelming movement that they are all gripped by at once. Such a space could only have been shaped by people who have quietly experienced within themselves what it means to have their own private spaces to live in and who feel themselves as isolated individuals who can become something "whole" without having to be associated with many others first. The space of their self-awareness has become so wide and so secure that it can now reflect their own being back to them.

People have been seized now by a passion for "interior space." They can no longer stand to be somewhere without being "inside." And so it happens that interior spaces are formed even in places where one is actually "outside": *yards* or *courts* become an important component of the architectural activity of this period. Every middle-class citizen, not to mention the nobleman and the prince, now builds his house in such a way that the structure as a whole encloses an additional interior space.

168

We have only to think of the narrow, compact, spaceless way in which the medieval town or castle was built to sense how everything widens out now from the inside. Suddenly everyone feels the need for space: private, bounded space in which he can breathe and whose boundaries are his own property because he has established them himself.

The town, as a single structural unit, is seized by this passion, too. As a form for the "inner space" of its self-awareness it creates the *market place*, with its arcades and colonnades, which is no more than a widened-out courtyard. All this is the product of nothing but a passion for inner space (Plate 49).

What this event means becomes even clearer if we connect it with the other stream of events south of the Alps, which did not come together with the northern stream until somewhat later. In the south, developments took a very different course. What happened there was not slow, organic growth but something that had more the character of a sudden, decisive break. This break is not as radical as it seems, of course, for the Renaissance merely reached back to an earlier stage of the same cultural epoch that had been the womb of what was new in the north.

In Italy the Romanesque and the Gothic never took hold quite as strongly as they did in Germany and France. They were always a little alien there, and whenever something special was to be built, artists were sent for from the north. The ruins of antiquity could still be found on all sides, not only in the country but in the people themselves.

When that deep and far-reaching transformation now began to take place in the human soul, it passed through Italy like a sigh of relief. For what had now to be said could be expressed much better through the classical heritage that lingered on in the depths of the southern blood than was possible with the forms the northern artist found so intractable as he struggled to wrest the new from them, often with such bizarre results. Suddenly, people felt the world of the Middle Ages as something foreign and unrelated. They shook it off, and their own powerful past took its place.

But what was expressed now only needed different words to say the same thing as what was struggling toward expression in the north: interior space. For the essential aspect of the Renaissance is not so much the fact that it rediscovered antiquity as the fact that it used the vocabulary of antiquity to say something new: self-contained, quiet, unified space. This was much easier, in a certain sense. The Greco-Roman column or

pillar had been the classical expression of supporting and sustaining. The coffered ceiling, the barrel vault, and especially the dome were a much more convincing solution to the problem than the decorated vault.

This is why the nature of the problem was also understood more easily and quickly, in a certain sense. The *central type* of building came to be preferred, and the representation there of the space that was self-aware and at rest within itself was the most perfect one of its age (Plate 50).

But inherent in all this was a danger of no small proportions. For the heritage that awoke here, even though not untransformed, was not the pure world of classical Greek culture, but the violent one of the Caesars. One can feel this very strongly. A will to power speaks from the buildings of this time, from the palaces of the noble families, which in their heavy, conscious bulkiness seem born from the spirit of the Roman triumphal arch, as well as from the churches, which should actually be serving a different god.

This is true even though in the Renaissance this world of the Caesars emerges transformed in more than one respect. Again and again we find this Caesar-like quality somewhat softened after all. Somewhere from the heavens of that time the smile of Saint Francis was still shining down in its infinite kindness and purity.

All the members and joints of this architecture have been experienced and worked through much more deeply and intensively than was the case in ancient Greece and Rome. Even though it is only slightly emphasized, there is also a central axis, like a backbone, and it has a point toward which the entire space is oriented and in which that space comes to a self-awareness that is often quite exciting: the High Altar. The cross, the intersection of nave and transept, the awareness that man is the place where two worlds interpenetrate, has been the great school whose fruits now become effective and visible in the creation of space. On every hand, laws are at work which can be, and have been, understood by man. Man does not live in the space alone, but in the pillars, the walls, the passages, the cornices and the capitals as well. He lives in them just as he does in the limbs of his own body.

This is what gives the Italian Renaissance its special flavor. The experience which gave rise to these spaces is the experience of the body in which we live and of the limbs in which our strength is active. It is the experience of bumping up against a boundary which is man himself.

Plate 49. Weil der Stadt. Market place with fountain, town hall and church.

171

Plate 50. Mantua, S. Andrea. Begun in 1472 from designs by Leon Battista Alberti.

And now it becomes clear what everything we have observed thus far really means. The interior space that man enters is man himself. He himself has become the house in which he lives. He no longer finds himself within the community, but within himself.

This is why all the "buildings" in which man has been sheltered up to now begin to fall apart: the church, the hierarchy of social classes, knighthood, the Empire. The cathedral, with its "additive" style, was the expression of group-like self-awareness, and as a house that concealed an infinite variety within its higher unity, it was the expression of both the structure and the feeling of the medieval world. Suddenly, the cathedral no longer exists. It is the individual who stands there now, completely on his own, thrown back onto and into himself. What is happening has been described thousands of times: the birth of individuality.

But this was a process that began entirely from within, and all the ex-

172

ternals, including the inventions, only expressed and aided it. Nothing reflects this growth of a new world-space from within outwards more clearly than the sculpture.

Sculpture

At the same time in which the hall church was coming into being, other spatial structures grew up inside it as smaller temples within the temple: the marvelously carved wooden altarpieces, the tabernacles and the pulpits. These are spatial structures, but they are actually born out of the sculpture, not the architecture.

As the pure expression of their essential nature, the Middle Ages created and carried the cathedral as a "total work of art," born out of the dim experience of the unity of all diversity in the fatherly ground of the world.

When the experience of this unity began to fade and the world seemed shattered and broken, men's attitude, the direction of their search for God, remained the same. The Gothic was the desperate attempt to regain the heaven that had been lost. This is why the Gothic still had the will to preserve the cathedral as a total work of art.

Now, however, as the new age dawns, the disintegration of the cathedral becomes complete. The spheres of the individual arts become independent. Each one seeks its own laws and strives to create a new totality out of itself. The earliest dramas come into being; these are "mysteries," or religious plays, at first, but performed outside the church. Then come the beginnings of artistic "worldly" music. Painting detaches itself from the walls and begins to be done on wooden panels. Finally, the sculpted figures which until now have been an integral part of the casings, portals, soffits and pillars of the architecture leave this womb, too.

Everywhere the same thing happens that has taken place in the human realm in general. The house that until now has sheltered everything individual within itself falls apart, and each individual finds "its own" house, or space in which to live.

For what is taking place now is a process involving many different worlds (*ein Weltenprozess*)!.

In Italy, once again, the new developments are immediately very decisive, leading to the creation of a completely free-standing sculpture in the round. But there, too, the first step, though taken only fleetingly, is the one which Germany, true to its own character, did not get beyond for a long time: the path to the altars, pulpits and tabernacles.

This development takes its start from the group sculpture, and from the relief in particular. Suddenly their individual figures, until now confined entirely within the surface, need more space for themselves, as well as an awareness of this space. They are no longer content to remain standing alongside each other in a single plane, but step behind or in front of each other. Moving farther apart, they also relax and become freer and freer. And this space which slowly grows around them is born from a new feeling of life they have within them; they breathe it out through all their limbs. What a great effort this is at first, and how small the space! But gradually it attains more depth, until in the end it flows widely and freely around the figures.

From the very beginning, this space has a boundary and attains a definite shape. This is what leads to the masterworks of the carved wooden altars. They arise, so to speak, from the need of the figures assembled within them to give a definite contour to this space which has grown out of them; from a need inherent in the space itself, in fact, whose particular character it is to be "inner space." This is the origin of the many deep and secret hollows of these altars, which are still closed off toward the front by dainty networks of lattices and tendrils (Plate 51).

Man has plunged into the element of inner space with his whole being. That is what these works proclaim.

In the area of sculpture, *Italy* again immediately departed more radically from its heritage, just as it had done in the area of architecture. Its most celebrated achievement was probably the "discovery" of the human body and of how man lives within his limbs.

It was a real discovery of a whole new land, which the artists entered in awe and amazement. Admiration of the human body had, of course, played a great role in Greek and Roman sculpture, but there the body had been entered from without, from the direction of the gods. Now, the

Plate 51. Creglingen, Tauber region. Centerpiece of the Altar of Mary by Tilman Riemenschneider. About 1505-1510.

174

artists enter it from within. The classical ideal was seen in looseness, relaxation, the free play of the limbs in accordance with their own inherent laws, moderation and freedom: the human body as a pure work of art, totally non-individual. Now, however, the stirring and inner tension of the individual are the very essence of the experience, along with the expression of the individual soul, the personal will and the particular destiny which each body constitutes for its bearer; not, in other words, the almost unself-conscious play of the body alone, but the self-conscious human being as he lives and moves within his body. In the ancient world man enjoyed the free play of the body as a work of art, made by the gods, but only recently released by them, from *their* hands. Now, man enjoys himself in his body. An individual consciousness fills this body to its very limits; in fact, these limits are where it lives. What is experienced now is not *the* human body with its broad range of possibilities, but rather the absolutely individual body as the house of the victorious, self-conscious personality.

Egypt experienced the *body inhabited by gods*. Greece experienced the body purely in itself as an art work of the gods, but one which had been set free from the sway of superhuman powers. Now, the experience of the *body inhabited by man* begins, seized and marked in its innermost core by the inscription of the character and destiny of its owner (Plates 52/53).

That was the deed and the nature of the Italian Renaissance. In *Germany*, things were quite different at first. The same polarity of the German and the Italian way of experiencing things which was so marked in their respective architectures shows up also in a specific aspect of German sculpture which has led to the most peculiar misunderstandings. We notice it in the exuberant growth of the garments that sets in now; the folds swell and grow into regular mountains of folds, becoming so full and densely packed that the figure itself is completely lost in them. Only the head, the hands and, at most, the feet can still be seen. But the body has completely disappeared in those masses of folds.

The experience of the uncovered body and of its structure, which was so significant in the Italian Renaissance, is simply not there; its very existence is denied outright. Had Italy long since heard the call of the new

Plate 52. Venice. Equestrian statue of Condottiere Bartolomeo Colleoni (1400-1475) by Andrea del Verrocchio (1436-1488).

176

age and obeyed it, while Germany was still stuck back in the Middle Ages?

These very mountains of folds are the strongest expression of the fact that a new world is dawning. They only say it in a more mysterious and symbolic way, and their message is only misunderstood because one keeps hearing the sound of Italy in the background.

These figures are firmly implanted in their garments as if they were in a house. They "live" in these garments. It is not a case of artistic inability or mere survival of outworn tradition. It may be a clumsy expression, but it is nevertheless a genuine expression of what is passing through these madonnas and saints, disciples, peasants and sages. It is a sense of infinite well-being, of *being entirely inside*. For the garments bulge out in such a way that they create space and use it to surround and envelop the figure they are hiding and protecting.

North and south of the Alps the same experience of entering inner space has opened up in people, and both architecture and sculpture express it in the same way. It is just that in Italy this experience goes straight into the will and is grasped and understood in a purely human way—too soon, we could almost say. In Germany, on the other hand, it is experienced with awe and wonder as an event of cosmic proportions under which men tend more to suffer than to rejoice, at least at first. Sensing the immeasurable responsibility it brings, they bear it as their destiny.

Painting

Medieval painting had been an art form concerned solely with the two dimensions of the planar surface. Nowadays we have so little feeling for what this means that we even lack the appropriate concepts to describe it with. We speak, for example, of the "gold background" behind its figures. But this is already not quite correct, for "background" is a concept derived from an aspect of spatiality which these pictures completely lack. These pictures have no foreground or background. In fact, there is no space in them at all. All the figures in them stand in spacelessness.

Plate 53. Detail of 52.

179

Now, however, this begins to change. The *picture surface* is transformed into the *picture space*, and all its figures—knights and saints, patriarchs, kings and bishops—step out of their spacelessness into space. This does not happen all at once. It takes a long time for this space to absorb the surface and take on real depth. But it begins everywhere at the same time. It is touching to see the artists of this period, especially the first ones, searching for this new element. Often they have no idea at all of what they really want, and so they grope around for it but fail to find it. The only thing certain is a deep inner urge that leaves them dissatisfied with all their past achievements. Ceaselessly they toil for every advance, and when, in death, they lay aside their brushes, they pass the task on to their sons; their grandsons will still have to struggle with it, even though by that time they will be able to look back over a good part of the journey.

There are many indications of how much this new sense of space owes its origin to the interior. The preference for painting interiors as such is only one such indication. Landscapes, too, are painted as though they were experienced as interior spaces. How enticing it would be to step into them and go for a stroll! Always they point into their own interior space, never actually out beyond it. In the background are mountains, or the facade of a house or temple; on the right and left, people or animals turn in toward the center; even in front, where the space opens out toward the viewer by necessity, it is still bounded by at least a staff to be stepped over, a bundle of straw to be cleared away or a bouquet of flowers to be admired before he can enter the actual picture space.

The same passion for interior space was what gave rise to the courtyards and town squares. In this way, interior space actually becomes an integral part of the outside world as well. It is a space born entirely from within. Ever more skillfully the master learns to guide his hands and brush, and through these this space grows over onto the canvas or the panel of linden wood. The master does not merely see it with his eyes but experiences it with his whole being.

Gradually the artists succeed in representing this space with a greater and greater depth, relaxation and sensitivity, until at last, in Dürer's *Hieronymus in the Cell*, we seem to hear the silence that permeates this room, breathe its air and feel the humanness that fills the space as if we could touch it. This room is inhabited and filled out to its very limits by the meditating saint. He even "inhabits" the lion and the dog; the books still remember that they were laid down only a short while ago; the skull knows that it is not just sitting on the window sill; the crucifix placed by his hand at the edge of the table forms a new, inner boundary. This whole festive room has come into being from "within" him, and his presence can be sensed not only in its innermost part but also at its outer limits. He is the kind master in this house; everything obeys him readily and willingly, waiting quietly to serve his slightest gesture, like the writing hand guided by the overflowing light shining within him. This is truly, in perfection, a human being—a "space"—with full self-comprehension and full self-awareness (Plate 54).

Another phenomenon becomes extremely significant now, especially when viewed within this context.

From generation to generation, in fact almost from decade to decade, we can follow the gradual disappearance of the gold foundation from the pictures and the gradual emergence of *the earth* from below. There are pictures that show an especially well-painted earth in their lower part, while the sky rising from the horizon is gold and will likely still be ornamented. The next step is represented by the pictures which show a blue sky above the earth, but over it—or behind it?—there is still a gold one. This goes on until the gold sky has completely disappeared and the entire picture space is filled with the earthly space and the blue sky that we see with our eyes. These are the pictures in which the figures, who until now have been floating in the spacelessness of the gold background, step down onto the earth.

But this is something they have to learn. At first they are very hesitant, standing there insecurely, hardly touching the ground beneath their feet. They are still completely weightless, and many times it would not surprise us if they simply took off and flew away. Sometimes, of course, they are wearing a garment of velvet or fur, and its natural weight is something of an embarrassment to them. But slowly their hesitant, uncertain placement becomes a conscious standing. Awareness of the earth moves into their feet, takes root in the earth and streams backward through their whole being. At this point they stand and are really there.

This is not only a matter of acquiring a new technique of painting. It is a concern of all mankind. *Man steps onto the earth.* We have to see very clearly that this is the first time man discovers the earth and really steps onto it. And if we never knew this before, we would be overcome

with amazement just to consider from how far away man has had to come to have to wander for so many thousands of years before his foot could arrive at this point. Never before had man portrayed this earth of ours for its own sake. It had never even entered into his consciousness. In Egypt man knew the gods, experienced the gods, walked among gods and nothing but gods, for whenever he chose to portray animal or plant forms they were the expression of divine life. In Greece and throughout the Middle Ages, man knew Man, and only Man. The Greek's "enjoyment of the senses" is no objection to this, for it too was directed only toward Man. Only now does man really open his eyes and look into the world of the earth.

But that is where he is now, filled with the joy of discovery. Not only the map of the geographers changes. New lands open up in every direction. The laws of the earth's physical nature are discovered. Modern science begins. The first of the inventions appear that will change the world. But it is quite possible that more was accomplished for all this discovery in the studios of the painters than anywhere else.

And what a wealth of discovery it is! There is not a picture from this period that does not contain at some point a proud and radiantly joyful report of some discovery or other. It may be a little bundle of straw that sticks out loosely over the edge of a roof; it may be a belt buckle or a blade of grass, a cooking-pot, a key bag, the heavy brocade of a priestly garment or a bean blossom—the infinite profusion of earthly phenomena is just there, waiting for man. And with what eagerness, what young and naive joy and thirst for adventure he rushes toward them! Indeed, the feeling of these *Meister Frankes* and *Meister Bertrams, van Eycks, Stephan Lochners, Meister Wilhelms, Konrad Witzes* and all the others, nameless or well known, was probably no less exalted than that of the men who discovered whole new parts of the earth. Nor were these silent discoverers of the earth any less bold.

Now what we are calling the "discovery of the earth" in its broadest sense is actually, in its deepest sense, an affair of the feet. The painters also did not carry out their expeditions with their eyes alone, but with their whole being, even as they sat quietly working away in their studios.

Plate 54. Albrecht Dürer (1471-1528). "Hieronymus in the Cell." Copper plate engraving from 1514.

Man "stepped onto" the things of the earth. He "moved over" them, experiencing them deeply. No matter what they paint, it is more than a mere visual impression; it is also not just something "grasped," but something that has been "stepped on." It is hard to find a more fitting characterization than this.

Especially characteristic of this kind of painting are the pictures, primarily by Dutch masters, which one is actually in the habit of calling "wander-pictures" ("Wanderbilder"): landscapes that lure the viewer into them on winding roads that lead to all kinds of people, strange places in the landscape, houses, rivers and groups of trees, to steep cliffs, up onto mountains and into valleys and forests. These landscapes beckon to us to "step" right into them and to become a part of the abundant variety of their life (Plate 55).

Another facet of this is that there is often a great expansiveness in the pictures of this period. Infinite distances are conjured up, while a "middle ground" is only barely suggested. At the same time, what is seen in the distance is painted with an exaggerated distinctness that the best eye could never perceive, no matter how clear the air.

This is not a mere shortcoming, a temporary unfamiliarity with the atmosphere and its laws which, a short while later, will be grasped in a very significant way. This phenomenon corresponds to the one in which interior space is projected outwards as well, distance itself becoming nearness, a nearness that is actually entered. Nothing tempts the artist to do this as much as what is farthest away.

It will now be clear what it means when we say that the organ man begins to take the world into himself with is his foot, which he uses to step onto the earth and all its phenomena. This gives us a faint idea of the cosmic character of the tremendous change which is taking place now from one age to the next. For this is nothing less than the earthly, human aspect of what can be called, from its cosmic aspect, the sun in Pisces.

In Egypt, man had experienced both himself and the center of the world in which he too was at rest as being under the divine influence of the cosmic Word. This was the sun in Taurus, the Bull. In Greece and throughout the whole of the Middle Ages, he derived a sense of security and certainty of soul from the act of understanding. This was the sun in

Plate 55. Adrian Isenbrant (about 1485-1550), Dutch painter. "Rest on the Flight to Egypt." About 1520. Munich, Alte Pinakothek.

Aries, the Ram. Now, however, the "organ" by means of which man stands within the world as a whole becomes the "encounter" of one being with another in its totality, the "entrance" of one being into another, the "personal" destiny that guides each one along his own particular path. This is the sun in Pisces, the Fishes.*

This shows itself in an elemental way in another change that the figures in the pictures undergo.

Throughout the Middle Ages, painting had maintained a character akin to that of writing, often with an incredible power of expression and in a sphere which was still a direct and powerful revelation of the spiritual world. This painting was full of symbols; in fact, it was almost nothing but a symbol, an indication of something else, never just a copy of this present world of ours. Its figures and events lived in eternity. The ones who bore the action withdrew completely behind the event, which was indicated by a few conventional gestures. The figures themselves were nothing, mere silhouettes of themselves, or hieroglyphs. The whole picture was nothing but a shadowy image of the real event, to which it pointed.

Now, all this changes. A mysterious process begins. Suddenly, all these figures are no longer satisfied with merely pointing to something; they want to be themselves. They begin to move from within themselves, stepping apart or coming together to form groups. All of a sudden, living faces break through the mask-like rigidity. Each one assumes his or her own individual role in what is going on. Although it is hard to say just exactly where the one stops and the other begins, we no longer find a picture simply saying that once upon a time there was this holy man who had such and such a thing happen to him. All at once he is right there himself, and we can look directly into the middle of what is happening. We experience it close-up, with all the excitement of its immediate presence. The pictures have become windows that we can look through into this presence as easily as looking into a neighbor's house.

The next step is that the patrons themselves, who commission the pictures, want to pass over into that space themselves and become an inte-

*Translator's note: The thinking in this passage is based on the traditional association of certain signs of the zodiac with specific areas of the human body; in these cases, Taurus with the throat and larynx, Aries with the head and brain and Pisces with the feet. The bull, the ram and the fishes are also archetypal images associated with the ancient Egyptian, ancient Greek and Christian cultures, respectively.

gral part of the picture's activity. Now, for instance, Chancellor Rolin can be seen in the same room in which the Virgin is sitting enthroned with her child. An angel hovers over her, holding a crown that is much too heavy over her head; the chancellor, meanwhile, has dropped reverently to his knees at his prayer desk (Plate 56).

This becomes very fashionable now. The eminent figures of this world make the saints come to them, lend them their own splendid garments and get them to recommend them to the divine majesty. Queen Anne of France, painted by the *Master of Moulins*, kneels down beside St. Magdalene, and in the painting by *Jean Fouquet*, Etienne Chevalier stands next to St. Stephen. Even the honorable *Mayor Meyer* of Basle has himself and his whole family painted at the feet of the Madonna, who is just stepping out of a niche, and *Archbishop Albrecht of Brandenburg* goes so far as to have himself painted at the feet of the Crucified One on Golgotha.

Of course, it becomes a fad, and not a harmless one. But the true and deeper reason for it is the boundless urge to bring all these figures and stories into the closeness of the present, into the here and now, and to meet them personally, as one ego to another. The desire is also there to "enter" the distance of some other event or destiny, another time, another human being.

This is what it means for man to enter into himself, or interior space— the new kind of cosmic space. This age gives away the most intimate secret of its evolution, however, in an image of mythical power and significance.

Myth

An image went through the Middle Ages, gathering around itself the whole fervor and devotion of these centuries: the image of the Virgin and the Child.

She was represented a thousandfold. She shone in the initials and illuminated pages of the missals and evangelistaries. She stood in the portals, lintels and walls of the cathedrals, as well as in chapels and crypts, chiseled in stone, carved in wood, luxuriously portrayed in mosaic, or

187

painted. Again and again it was this same picture, but in the course of centuries it underwent a significant change.

At first she was a sublime and distant goddess. Austere or mild—either way, she was unapproachable. But then, ever so slowly, she came closer to man. She inclined her head, which at first had been so stern. In her countenance there appeared a smile of infinite sweetness. Tenderly she laid her cheek against her child's. Closer and closer she came to man, gathering up her garment and arranging it in beautiful folds.

Always, however, she is lost in herself or in her child, or absorbed in her own great sorrow or in the tender sadness of her own good fortune. Or, stern and sublime, her gaze is directed into a greater world on beyond man. She is near men, but not yet with them. With her child and yet a little beyond him, she is like someone quietly anticipating some momentous event. Throughout the whole Middle Ages, not a single Madonna can be found who is already looking at her child.

Now, however, this pure bud opens out into an infinite radiant blossom. One single scene from her life stands out in all its power: the birth of the child. Now she comes to man; indeed, to all men. Into the wretched hut she comes, into the palace and the temple, the burgher's house, the garden and the forest; to peasants and priests, the high-born and the humble, dignified councilmen and simple-minded maidens—who can count them all as they stand and kneel there in these pictures, fold their hands, take fright and rejoice and fall silent in their devotion?

And then she raised her eyes to look directly at whoever comes and stands in front of her. What a confrontation there is in this look of the Sistine Madonna's! She is "there" now, she and her child with his infinite eyes. Long in her coming, she has arrived at last (Plate 57).

She was the mystery which hovered over the whole of the Middle Ages. But even then she had been on her way for a long time. She had passed through Greece as Demeter, and from there she brought with her the ears of grain on her garment. Even earlier, she had wandered through Egypt as Isis. That journey is the source of the moon at her feet. At that time she was a promise and a yearning. Now she is fulfillment.

We see her path: she comes down to us from the stars. For who would not believe that the crescent of the moon, the sphere closest to our own,

Plate 56. Jan van Eyck (1390-1441). "Madonna of Chancellor Rolin." About 1430. Paris, Louvre.

189

was only the threshold where she first became visible? Then she strode on through the waving fields of grain, and her goodness was felt in all that surrounded the earth in a cloak of etheric life. Now she has entered the very "house of man."

It is the path of the human soul, the history of its transformations through thousands of years.

In Egypt her range was very broad: from cosmic realms down to the great threshold itself. In Greece, the "veils" of columns around the temples, the rippling garments around the statues and the whole rapturous experience of form and beauty proclaimed her "comprehending" existence in the sphere of the creative forces of life which give birth to the physical, molding and shaping it as they stream around it. Now she has stepped onto the earth itself. What else is the "discovery of the earth" but this: that the human soul opens its eyes for the being and the laws of the earth?

This can also be seen as the path from Galilee, or Nazareth, full of life and surrounded as it is by mysteries of the etheric, to the rocky and purely earthly Judea, or Bethlehem,[13] the very place where the child is born in its earthly house.

It is the path of the human soul. And the child *is* born, at just that time and in just that place. This is why the age is filled with such tremendous Christmas joy. It seems now like a single, grand Christmas celebration. For the people of that time, the Christmas picture is *the* image of God. Again and again they paint it. Wood carvers and sculptors depict it. Christmas plays and Christmas carols ring out, and their glow and their sound have come all the way down to us. Who is it, then, who was really born there?

Blooming, fragrant flowers surround this child, and he radiates a magic charm of life. Heavenly songs ring out around him, too (Plate 58), and from him comes a heavenly light that beautifies the rough, simple faces of the peasants bending over him. In this light, the candlelight of an apprehensive Joseph or of the man praying quietly at his desk pale as if it were the sun.

It *is* the sun: its song, the resounding cosmic Word, its life-awakening magic; the sun's radiant light, inexhaustibly reproducing itself; the sun in

Plate 57. Raphael, actually Raffaelo Santi (1483-1520). "Sistine Madonna." About 1515-1519. Dresden.

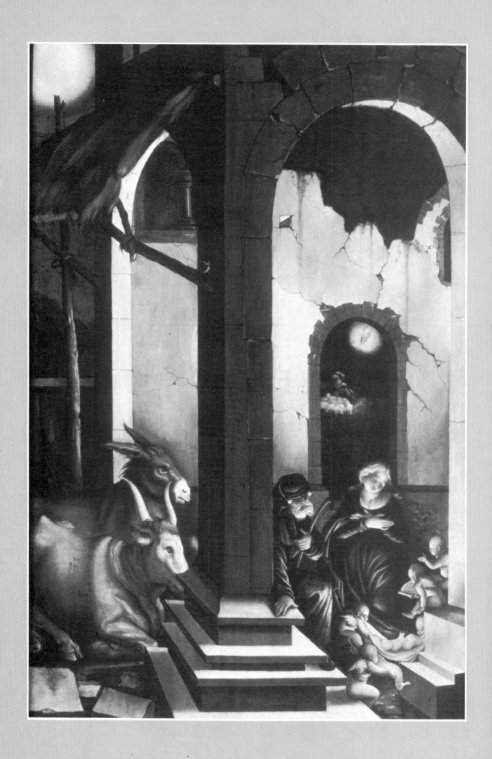

the house. Its journey from the sea onto the land and into the house, the long journey from Egypt, is over.

Osiris had died. Outside he could no longer be found. But he had sealed up his strength and his very being in the virgin, the human soul. Some day she would give birth to Horus. For thousands of years she carried him, overshadowed by his mystery. Now she has carried him to full term and given birth to him in the house.

It is the same house, the same space, that man went into in this age: man himself. God has entered him. God is rising in him like the sun. He is Immanuel, or "God in our midst."

Everyone in those days had a premonition of Him. Luther sensed Him when he felt compelled to obey what had dawned within him, in the face of everything that was held up to him from the outside as the centuries-old authority of a binding divine revelation.

Everyone who had "entered" the interior space of the earth built temples to Him: architects, sculptors and painters.

Hutten's jubilant remark, "It is a joy to be alive . . . ," was actually meant for Him.

From now on, man is the space where God rises into the world.

The sun in the house. We need to consider this image more closely, for there is something peculiar about the house in which this overwhelming event took place, and its peculiarity was equally and very distinctly emphasized by all the artists who represented it.

This house is a ruin. The roof, the walls and the openings of the doors and windows have been dilapidated and crumbling away for a long time now. Moss and grass have taken over and are burrowing deeper into cracks and joints.

Everyone shows this. Only the degree of decay differs from master to master. Sometimes it is a hut, still in fairly good condition. But sometimes it is the ruin of an enormous palace or temple. Great stone arches stretch up helplessly into the air. Here and there the layout of a large number of rooms can be seen, indicated almost solely by the remains of their foundations. Others are hinted at which, broken up, buried and forgotten, have long since disappeared. At one time, this "house" was a structure of great dignity and splendor, but now . . .

Plate 58. Hans Baldung, named Grien (1484-1545). Pupil of Dürer. "The Birth of Christ." 1520. Munich.

This is not just something taken over dogmatically from some external tradition. It is a real experience. We have to look and see for once how dusk and darkness crouch in corridors and corners, how decay prowls around everywhere and dust trickles down as everything crumbles away. This is experienced, experienced from within.

It is something sinister. But it is also the only way to understand a figure like *Hieronymus Bosch*. He, too, painted a Christmas scene, but everywhere in it we see ghosts, lunatics and demons peering through cracks and window openings, over the matted roof and around the rotting beams. The same gruesome ghosts populate all his pictures, his sinister houses, tree stumps, nooks and crannies, lurking everywhere, ready to emerge without warning from every human surrounding. They are most ghastly when there is no way to see them right away. How frightening the gesture of such a house is with its windows and doors that yawn open like empty eye sockets that keep on staring out of their emptiness, or like the spiteful, toothless mouth of some horrible, cowering ghost (Plate 59).

This experience was depicted in its most elemental way, however, by *Matthias Grünewald* in the Christmas picture of the Isenheim altar, the same picture in which the music of heaven resounds more sweetly and fully and the roses have opened with a purer and more delightful fragrance than in any other. This was the picture in which he put into the hands of the most blessed of all madonnas ever painted the ragged loin cloth of the Crucified One as the swaddling clothes in which she carries the child. This cloth is haunted by the greenish shadows of decay and is so rotten that we can only be amazed that its tatters still hold together and have not already crumbled away to dust (Plate 60).

The house in which the child is born, this earthly house of ours, is filled and dominated and hopelessly permeated by *death*. This is the experience that speaks to us out of all these pictures. This house is a grave, and the birth of the child is already the beginning of his passion. The whole earth is filled with death.

This is why the great *dance of death* is now experienced everywhere, that horrid rattling of bones that climb up out of their graves, dragging the air and the dread and the darkness up out of the depths and breathing it out over all the earth. *Dürer* saw the bony man of death as the crowned

Plate 59. Hieronymus Bosch (1450-1516). "Adoration of the Magi."

194

king of the earth, riding along on his lean, dead-tired mare, breathing paralysis wherever he appears. No matter how slowly he rides along, he will still show up everywhere, carried along by the mechanical trot of his terrible beast (Fig. 12).

Fig. 12. "Dance of Death," by A. Koburger, active in Nuremburg from 1440 to 1513.

He is everywhere. The more abundant and luxurious life appears to be, the more voluptuously he buries his teeth in the lips of this blossoming figure, now grown numb with horror. This is what *Hans Baldung Grien* envisioned (Plate 61).

There is no one he did not accompany or lie in wait for until the moment when he could step forward in all his gruesomeness: emperor and

Plate 60. Matthias Grünewald (about 1470-1528). "Mary and the Child" from the Isenheim Altarpiece. Painted about 1515 for the monastery of the Order of St. Anthony in Isenheim. Colmar, Museum.

king, pope and bishop, knight and shopkeeper, man and woman, councillor and peasant—no one who did not have death as his companion. But how long has this been the case? When Adam and Eve were driven out of Paradise, he was waiting at the gate, as *Hans Holbein* pictured it in his "Great Dance of Death."

This is the fulfillment of what Egypt had foreseen, of what it knew as inevitable destiny when it stepped on the threshold and of what it represented in the pylon of the temple, in the myth of the revolt of man and in its whole history. In Egypt it was still myth. Now it becomes reality. Just as man has now arrived at the "inner space" which has been his goal ever since Egypt, he has also arrived at the whole, relentless, gruesome reality of death.

Death goes wandering over the earth, and the rattling of his bones becomes the music of life. That is what this age experiences. But where does this experience come to men from? Where did one meet this figure face to face?

The image is an exact depiction of the point which man's consciousness has reached in the course of its development. Those centuries are, after all, the ones in which the age of thinking began, as well as that kind of consciousness which produced the great inventions. But that was only possible because man began to experience the physics and mechanics of the "bone-man" in the very depths of his being. This is why man was at first so mistrustful of the new world that was just coming into being. Deep down he knew that the "bone-man" was climbing up out of the darkness and that the dance of death was beginning.

For a short while this mistrust remained alive and acted as a warning. Then came the time when man became intoxicated with "progress" and forgot his hesitation. Today he is again beginning to see more clearly that at that time powers of the deep were actually starting to surface in a form of consciousness which—albeit in grandiose fashion—was only able to comprehend the world of death. This consciousness could only grasp the purely earthly part of man, that part of him related to the animal, and it only experienced the cosmos as a complicated accumulation of physical and chemical, that is to say, mechanical processes. This began with the advent of the Copernican planetary system. Between it and the dances of

Plate 61. Hans Baldung, named Grien (1484-1545). "The Kiss of Death." 1517. Basel, Kunsthalle.

198

death there is a close causal connection. Death grows, out into the whole cosmos, and as it does so, the universe becomes a dark and yawning grave.

The birth is the beginning of the passion. But the passion is also the birth of a new world. This, too, no age ever experienced to such a degree as this one. True, the house this child is born into is a house of death, but this child is the conqueror of death, from within outwards, in that he follows death right on into his house.

The very masters who were most shaken by their experience of the reality of death were also the ones who experienced the miracle of its overcoming in the most exalted way. How the mild and yet almost unbearable light radiates from the child in the many Christmas pictures of Hans Baldung Grien; the same is true of pictures by *Bartholomäus Bruyn, Albrecht Altdorfer* and many others. How everything blossoms around the child! What heavenly music resounds! Within this most tender of all beings there dawns an immeasurable strength, in the very midst of this dilapidated, crumbling house of death. The sun shining within it is stronger than death.

And in men the "mystery of the kneeling one" dawns, about which Rilke, in a marvelous letter to Ph. R. (Christmas, 1923), says that he who kneels will become greater than he who remains standing. These people with their simple, furrowed, bony faces—often true houses of death—how there dawns in them the miracle of an entirely new, unknown, as yet hardly imaginable life which reaches far beyond them.

The most magnificent painting of what was happening now was done by Grünewald, the very one who had used the swaddling clothes to weave the birth and the passion together in such a mysterious way. What he painted was the completion of birth, in that the "last house" to be entered is death—the grave. And he painted the resurrection, the overcoming of death, as a sunrise. For the radiant aura which surrounds the Risen One in his picture is the aura of the sun. The sun is rising—out of the earth (Plate 62).

This is the completion, but also the continuation, of the image of the sun in the house. It is the mystery that now begins to shine and also

Plate 62. Matthias Grünewald (about 1470-1528). "Resurrection." Isenheim Altarpiece, right panel. Visible together with the "Birth" and "Entombment" pictures when this panel is open.

begins to be sensed: the mystery of the earth, that the earth is the place of a mighty sunrise. This is the thought which from now on will give the greatest and deepest thinkers the feeling, "For my sake, be faithful to the earth!" For in the earth you remain faithful to the sun.

This is the great reversal, the re-evaluation of all values. The earth is the place of a sunrise. But also, the place where the sun rises is the earth. In former times, whoever sought the heart of the world had to raise himself up far into the distance. Now, the mystery of nearness begins. "The Kingdom of Heaven has come *near*." This did not happen only once, for those three years. It is still going on. He said, after all, "Lo, I am with you always. . . ."

VIII

THE MYSTERY OF THE EARTH

From the Baroque to Modern Times

The development of art in the centuries following the Renaissance has to be seen as the unfolding and assimilation of that impulse which had still come to Renaissance man like a gift of the gods. It had come to him with the magic of a first love and in such profusion that as yet it could not be understood in its totality at all; at first, it could not even be taken hold of. Even this seed had to die, so that the essence which it contained could develop further.

Experiences rapidly declined to the level of superficiality, a process which can be observed quite clearly. But the forceful sprouting of something new can also be discerned within and underneath this dying process. It is evident already in the Baroque and even more so in the painting of the Romantics. It undergoes one metamorphosis after another as it grows on powerfully into the future, the irresistible advance of the innermost impulse of the Renaissance which had revealed itself in Grünewald's picture of the Resurrection as the sunrise out of the earth.

In the Renaissance a process had begun in which the individual faculties of the human soul divide. The great chaos that results from this comes more and more into focus in these centuries, as science, art and religion move farther and farther apart. Science increasingly forgets how to look for God; religion loses its connection with the world-awareness that gradually arises out of science; and art begins to forget that it stands under the aegis of the saying, *numine afflatur*, meaning, "The sacred awe one feels for the depths of the Godhead wafts through its breath," as Raphael could still write in the Stanza della Segnatura. Art begins to forget that it, too, has a part in the revelation of the mysteries of the world. The great, universal secularization begins. The princes of this

203

world take possession of what had belonged to the church and had some-how really belonged to God, including areas and spaces that cannot be measured out and located on a map. The religious communities, how-ever, withdraw into areas that are ever more limited and meager, and the most they can do is to keep up a certain external appearance of cultural leadership in the face of competition from the rulers of the other areas. They cannot step out of the structure of the Middle Ages. Even the reformers, who undertook the whole bold venture, shrank back at the half-way point; the Reformation remained unfinished.

The whole fabric of life had hopelessly disintegrated. It is true that a few courageous individuals, especially in the age of Romanticism, tried to bring about a reconciliation and a new beginning. But their success, at least externally, was insignificant at first.

Now, *that* power which until then had been the servant of all the others usurps the leadership: science. In it and through it intellectualism and materialism raise their heads higher and higher. Already in the Ba-roque the capacity to take a higher reality into one's consciousness is ex-tinguished. The only thing still known is the earth. This is why, with very few exceptions, the pictures and sculptures of this period which depict heavenly scenes or saints are so untrue and unbearably fake. In these figures, which are so intoxicated with their own feeling, sentimen-tality and false pathos celebrate orgies of indecency. For these pictures are looking for a heaven that no longer exists, and they look for it in a place that can no longer even be found.

The only thing the people of this time know—and want—in the depths of their being is the earth. And even this they only know in part. For now that they are no longer able to comprehend the mysteries of their un-conscious depths, they are like children who have found golden utensils and the most precious stones and are playing with them, unaware of the treasures they have in their unheeding hands. They are like sleepwalkers who follow impulses they know nothing about, or dreamers whose dreams are grotesque and foolish caricatures of experiences of tremen-dous magnitude. But it is something tremendous which these souls are following at a barely conscious level. As a result, this age is full of the most grotesque misunderstandings, experiences which it can no longer, or not yet, understand. Now and then, of course, someone awakens to their deeper reality. Jakob Böhme, the "Philosophus teutonicus," was one of these; later on, it was the Romantics. From then on there are more and more in whom a consciousness awakens for the mystery in which man stands. We today are still engaged in the struggle to find it.

Baroque

The transition from the Renaissance to the Baroque is calm and hardly noticeable. It is a very quiet and organic process. But what is really happening?

One way to characterize this change has been to say that suddenly beauty no longer means harmony but strength. Harmony is a state of being, something resting quietly within itself, balanced and clarified. Strength is a state of becoming, something pressing out beyond itself, limitless and in constant ferment. This expresses itself in *architecture* more strongly than anywhere else.

The structural masses have been seized by a tremendous movement. There is not a single surface, line, column, capital, door lintel, window-sill or any other part of the building that has not been drawn into this process. Balconies, portals, open flights of steps leading up to a building, the enclosures of large public squares, everything swings in and out in magnificent curves. Wherever possible, the right angle, the square and the circle are suppressed and the ellipse, the parabola and the hyperbola are preferred (Plate 63).

Everything is transition, a striving for totality and wholeness and for the shaping of each individual part out of this wholeness and uniformity which transcends all limits.

The origin of the one as well as of the other is interior space. It is the element that has begun to move and permeates everything now. The movement of the surfaces and lines of the body of the building is secondary; it is only following the movement of the interior space. This, experienced as a living being, is what is really breathing in and out, swelling and receding, "sending" some spaces forth out of itself and drawing others back in (Plate 64).

Never before had there been an "inner space" in which it was possible to feel so centered, confirmed and uplifted. To be sure, these spaces—

205

churches as well as palaces—crave not so much the single individual who might like to spend a quiet hour in them as they do a festive crowd. But this should be a crowd that gathers around a single person who is the lord and king of the festival and in whom the whole affair reaches a peak of self-awareness. They are spaces meant for a prince and the royal household that swarms around him, growing over and enhancing him like a cloak. This is not only true for the great palaces of this era but also for its churches, in the same way. They too are spaces for magnificent, ecstatic festivals. Their prince is the priest, who holds the monstrance in his hands.

What begins to happen here in the Baroque can be described by saying that now the interior space begins to grow, not in the sense of an increase in its external size, but in such a way that the Renaissance space, resting quietly and securely within itself, begins to swell as though taken hold of by mysterious forces of life, like a seed that is just about to sprout.

This is why "beauty suddenly means strength." For this growth of interior space is a world-process, not one brought about by man but one which works through him; he only feels it working and "gives it space."

It is the age of absolute monarchy and the order of the Jesuits. And it is no accident that both of these institutions, even outwardly, became strong supporters of the new style, at least in architecture. For this growth of interior space is just what both proclaim by their very natures, even though they distort and misunderstand it.

When Louis XIV—*le roi soleil!* or "Sun King!"—said, *l'état c'est moi!* (I am the State!"), and this remark, to use an expression of Goethe's, marked the beginning of a new epoch, it was without a doubt the most despotic form of hubris conceivable. But it was nevertheless based on a genuine experience; otherwise he could never have carried it out the way he did. This experience was, that the human ego, man's own inner space, begins to grow out beyond him and that within his ego a larger and more encompassing one begins to find itself and shed its light.

When the Jesuit Order exerts all its energy to lead the power and the splendor of the church as an earthly institution to new and unknown heights, this is the most frightful misunderstanding of the Mystery of

Plate 63. Dresden, Zwinger, 1711-1722, from designs by D. Pöppelmann. Enclosed pavilion by B. Permoser.

207

Golgotha which has ever occurred. And yet behind this too is the premonition that the "Gloria Dei," the radiant sheen of God's revelation, is beginning to dawn out of the earth, that it must be found here and now and that a festival is beginning to spread over the entire earth.

A festival. There is a sense that something great is dawning, a treasury of new and infinite wealth that unites everything individual and separate. The brief centuries of the Renaissance were, no doubt, a time when it was "a joy to be alive." But this joy was always tempered by the realization that finding oneself also means finding death; that becoming an ego means, first of all, poverty and loneliness. This was readily admitted. But now something new is stirring, and it becomes more and more intense. If it is not a genuine awareness, it is at least a deep premonition of the fact that this death has been overcome.

Interior space begins to grow, but not just the individual space within itself. Growing out beyond itself, it begins to speak with other spaces, to sense and to affirm their existence as self-contained spaces. And yet it goes on to overcome all this. We can experience this in the great *staircases* of this period. These stairs have not been built just to meet a practical need. They are a metaphysical event. With the soaring melody of their magnificent flourish they lift themselves over distances which are more than merely measurable. Their direction always follows broken or irrational lines, and they always lead somewhere through spacelessness, out of rational spatiality. They also always contain an element of "turning around" or of "turning toward each other," an inner path and an inner meeting, the seriousness of encounter, but its joy as well. As they ascend, all weight is overcome (Plate 65; Fig. 13).

In *painting*, the same experience gives rise to those charming "interiors," especially among the Dutch (Plate 66). It is their charm, too, that the spaces they depict point beyond themselves and into others as a door opens into an adjoining room, and through curtains, alcoves and niches groups of spaces come about that do not just stand side by side but open toward each other. It is this play of spaces that charms and stirs the soul.

Now, however, it becomes even more significant when not only another interior space but the outside world itself "intrudes," through a

Plate 64. Ulm, Wiblingen Monastery. Library inside the abbey building. Built from 1714 to 1760 by Christian Wiedemann.

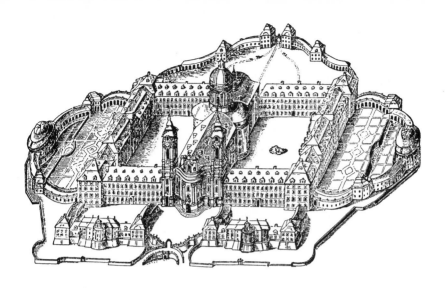

Fig. 13. Drawing of the Weingarten Monastery from the year 1723.

half-open window, say, or even a translucent one. Whenever this occurs, doors and windows take on an even stronger "threshold" character than if they would merely lead from one interior space to another. For even though the outer world is something alien, "otherness" itself, it is still waiting to be entered so that it, too, may become interior space. Interior space is growing out into the external world.

At this point we must take another look at the archetypal gesture of architecture: the way it soars upward in spaces, surfaces and lines.

Gothic architecture was also in motion, toward a specific goal. Everything streamed forward to the altar and upward into dizzying heights. Both kinds of movement had the same intent, to take heaven by storm and to conquer the bolted gates of Paradise. Our question now must be whether the mobility of Baroque space has some goal beyond itself in mind. Does it, too, seek to open up some hidden heaven?

This movement takes its start from *inner* space. For wherever a curve proceeds in such a way that it draws back into an interior, it is clear that it is not being pressed in from the outside but sucked in from the inside, by inner *space*, for the movement is three-dimensional. The lines and surfaces are only following the swelling and breathing of this space, but

Plate 65. Schöntal, staircase inside the monastery. 1707-1736, from designs by Johann Leonard Dientzenhofer with the assistance of Balthasar Neumann.

211

from the pattern of their movement it becomes apparent where this space is heading.

The basic pattern of this movement, which recurs in the foundation, the surfaces and all individual forms, is this:

It undergoes a thousand variations, through curves into angles and points, but always its form remains, difficult to grasp in mathematical terms and leading into the realm of the irrational.

It is none other than the lemniscate,

that archetypal figure described by Goethe in his poem, "Epirrhema":

> "Nothing's inside, nothing's outside,
> For what's inside's also outside.
> So, do grasp without delay
> Holy open mystery."

If we have experienced Baroque architecture inwardly, we understand its innermost secret, and as we stand facing it we will probably even feel like proclaiming this "Holy open mystery!" aloud. For this is the very goal of its movement, its swelling out and being sucked in, its yearning to go out beyond itself on the strength of its increasing self-containedness. This space yearns to reach out into the outer world, as space and as interior space. It wants to draw the outer world into its own inner being and somehow extract an inwardness from it.

The heaven that this architecture wants to open up is not in some far-off Beyond; it is the heaven that lies open all around us, the one we live in the very midst of without our knowledge. It is the inner space of the earth, and even though it is hidden in every flower, every stone and every leaf, in the depths of our being we sense it standing open, waiting.

Without realizing it, the painting of this period betrays the presence of this heaven as well.

Renaissance painting had really managed to grasp the form, the sub-

Plate 66. Pieter de Hooch (1629-1677). "The Mother at the Cradle." 1659-1660. Berlin, Kaiser Friedrich Museum.

213

stance, the color and the contour of the earth. Strongly and clearly outlined, each individual object glowed with its own being. In the Baroque, however, something else is "discovered," weaving between the individual objects. Another element, equally essential, is discovered as well, namely, haziness, the misty, cloudy quality of the atmosphere and its phenomena.

On the one hand, this way of painting expresses the experience of the density of space and of the tendency of space to integrate its individual components into itself, an experience which came out strongly in the architecture. On the other hand, it leads through all these elements to the formation and discovery of what "painting" really is. Indeed, we have to say that the Baroque discovers a whole new world of *colors*.

The colors of the Renaissance were basically still those of the Middle Ages, the same strong, clear, somewhat hard tones that had been in use for many centuries. But now they have an entirely different glow about them. Colors have been found to have a life and value, a quality of "colorfulness" all their own, a vitality of glowing and fading, a way of merging into each other, arising out of light and being swallowed up again in darkness.

Suddenly the earth has colors that play over softly into one another, colors that blossom in the light and burn with an inner fire. Everything is aglow, the leaves of the trees, blossoms and fruits, the clouds in the sky, human skin, fabrics and various kinds of wood. The whole infinite variety of earthly phenomena lights up, and the eye is soon drunk from the floods of color. For all the colors seem secretly suffused by a golden glow that breaks loose every so often and pours out in a powerful flood. It is as though the gold background that had dissolved in the Renaissance as the earth ascended is suddenly present again, but now it is within the earth, blossoming forth out of every facet of it.

In medieval painting the presence of the gold background was natural and unquestioned. Now, the gold is no longer simply there but begins to glow, born for the first time from the dramatic element of light. The radiance of this gold shines up out of the darkness of the earth.

Nowhere do we see this appearing as clearly as in the paintings of *Rembrandt*. As faces, gestures and objects come to birth there out of impenetrable shadows, glow gently, are there and fade away again, we feel how all his pictures are really visions of his inner nature, glowing in a mysterious light whose source remains unseen because it lies within his

214

own inner self. Rembrandt's whole passionate participation in the birth of this inner light has passed over into the light of his paintings and has become nothing but light, creative, regenerative light, wresting form from darkness (Plate 67).

The secret gold foundation of everything earthly is gleaming upwards in this light, but also in the activity of the viewer and in his active devotion. Here, too, it is the inner space of man which is growing out beyond man himself. It is the first, distant glimmer of a fact, hardly grasped at all as yet, to which human consciousness was nevertheless soon to awaken: man's responsibility toward the earth. For heaven can only dawn out of the earth by passing through man himself.

There is a hint of this heaven in another phenomenon, even though this phenomenon tends more to keep it hidden than to reveal it. The principle that energy is more important than harmony can be recognized in the motifs chosen for the visual arts of sculpture and painting as well. These are the pictures in which people with wine-reddened faces revel in festive exuberance, making noise, singing, dancing, fighting and enjoying all stages of drunken bliss. But they are also the gigantic paintings from the studio of *Peter Paul Rubens* with their overflowing profusion of swelling, blossoming nakedness. Of course one can have one's doubts about the artistic value of these things, but what they reveal, though veiled, is still of great significance. For in all this there is much more than mere clumsy materialism and a coarse voluptuousness. In the overbrimming fullness of life these pictures display, there sounds the same intoxicating music that plays through all the life of that age; in the sculpture it creates those swelling, storm-inflated garments and the pathos which we moderns can hardly endure and lives itself out in the preference for mythological scenes with their gods and heroes. In the final analysis, it is the same music that resounded in the architecture of that period as well. It is like a plunge into the primal forces of the living, the gentle washing of a cosmic life onto the shore of the earthly. It is no accident that music in particular blossomed so magnificently in just this period as well. The resounding of the cosmic Word begins to dawn now and be heard, within the earth (Plate 68).

What is unfolding now as the basis of all the phenomena described is the path *from the house up onto the mountain*, the fulfillment of the mystery of Christ's resurrection in the Ascension.

The heaven into which Christ disappeared was not in some far-off

215

Beyond. This heaven rose within the earth. The clouds that received Him and concealed Him within themselves were not at a measurable border of the earthly realm. They were the eternally changing, fertile, etheric spheres of life that bear within them both blessing and wrathful judgment. The "transfiguration of earthly being by the being of heaven" is the mystery of the Ascension.

The path "to the Father" can be understood this way as well, as a mystery. It is quite exact to say that the Father is found in nature, in all created things, in the broad reaches of the outer world; it is the nature of the Son, however, to be "inside," to be found within the Ego. This way of stating it expresses the basic elements of what in those days so stirred the souls of men. Interior space is growing; this is the yearning for the Ascension, the longing to return all things to the Father through the Son. The light grows on, into the dim twilight of everything "cloudlike." This is the longing for the transfiguration of earthly being and for the heaven that stands open within the earth and grows and grows.

What takes place at that time is something unheard of. Who among the people of that time has any idea of the majesty of this event? It takes place like the rising of the outer sun, unconcerned whether people see it or not. They are asleep, but sleeping, they all follow the mysterious whisper that touches them. The depths of contemporary philosophy are also stirred by the same problems as architecture, for instance. Its thought "structures," such as those of Leibniz, Descartes and Spinoza, bear within themselves the same spaces that swell up so with life, the same flourish as the staircases. They, too, are searching from one interior space to the next.

Now and then, however, the flashing lightning would wake someone up. One of the very few was Jakob Böhme, who wrote a book which he called *Aurora or the Coming of the Dawn* and another one called *Mysterium Magnum (The Great Mystery)*. Böhme was somewhat aware of the mystery of the earth, but his work did not have much effect. He himself was thus only a single flash of the tremendous event that was pressing toward the light in the Baroque and eventually worked its way into the life of dreams, where Romanticism became the first to awaken to it.

Meanwhile, the shadows cast by the light that was dawning grew, and with the steady growth of intellectualism and rationalism these shadows became denser and denser.

Plate 67. Rembrandt, actually R. Harmensz van Rijn (1606-1669). "Entombment of Christ." 1653. Dresden.

Romanticism

The form the Baroque assumes in the years of its decline is a clear indication of the weakening of its creative energies. The *Rococo*, which should be carefully distinguished from the late German Baroque, is no longer capable of creating great architectural forms. Only as interior decoration does it adorn the festive halls of the fashionable world with its airy playfulness. It is purely a "surface" art and, as such, a very charming one. Yet there is no doubt that beneath this "surface" greater depths are hidden than one would like to admit; often enough its cheerfulness is the heroic mask of a profound melancholy, of a world that senses it is doomed to die as it dances gaily over its own graves.

For the philosophy of this age is rationalism, the Enlightenment. It is a "surface" philosophy in the same way as the Rococo is a "surface" art. People are still "witty"; there is still a heritage to squander. But for how much longer? Soon, *"l'homme machine"* will no longer have any *"esprit"* about him.

Art degenerates to mere decoration of the social life. Fashionable portraits, scenes from the theater in which this society continually indulges, these are the tasks art now sets itself.

The French Revolution, which put an end to all this, was the grave one had dug for oneself, for it came about under the sign of freedom and reason which this very society had raised aloft in its own salons. In actual fact, the revolution was a suicide.

With this a great heritage had been squandered, the heritage of classical antiquity which the Renaissance had come into. Until now, this heritage had always been taken for granted as a source of inspiration; though not always sought, it was also an authority that had never been questioned.

The new era begins to wake up to itself. For a long time motherly forces have nourished and protected it, but have also kept it veiled; now it has shaken them off. A growing number of people feel something quite new in the air as the old ideals begin to become barren and new, creative forces no longer seem to stream in from the past but only from the future. To be sure, these decades also see the rise of *Classicism*. But it,

Plate 68. Peter Paul Rubens (1577-1640). "The Last Judgment." About 1615. Munich, Alte Pinakothek.

too, is a whole new, independent struggle to come to grips with antiquity, born from the forces of consciousness and permeated by consciousness, and it does not come out of the tradition of the Renaissance (Plate 69).

This is the significance of *Romanticism*: it is the awakening, or more precisely, the struggle to awaken into a world that has long since reached its present state of growth and has actually been all around man for a long time.

Man awakens, into God's return. How great God had been in Egypt, when all the spaces of the earth were filled with His presence and the earth and man were but a province of the cosmos filled with His breath. Egypt, however, experienced man's great fall into sin, God's withdrawal from this world and the transformation of the earth into an empty, godless desert. Godless it then remained, and man was abandoned, for thousands of years. Now, God rises again, and the earth becomes the first province of a new, God-permeated cosmos. This it becomes through man, who awakens to a sense of his highest dignity through the realization that he is the place where a new and future world is being formed. This is the meaning of Novalis's mysterious sentence: "We are on a mission—*we are called to form the earth.*"

What the Romanticists "discovered" was *the landscape*: not landscape as a framework and a setting for human beings and human events, but as something existing in its own right, worthy of being looked at and represented purely for its own sake. From this we can see what distinguishes these pictures from earlier "pure" landscapes. These exhausted themselves in representing what was visible and physical. Suddenly it happens that what is visible is only the foreground for something invisible, and what is physically objective only serves to conceal something much more essential which is far greater than man.

It is like the fairy tales which the Romantics loved so much, where the maid, who has to do all the dirty work and sit quietly in the corner, unnoticed by everyone, suddenly turns out to be the daughter of the king. It is like waking up, opening one's eyes and stepping out into a whole new world which at last is the "real," genuine, true reality that has only been misunderstood for so long. This was how people felt now. Fully aware that they were laying bare the foundations of a new world era, they nevertheless preserved a deep reverence for the past. For this very future

Plate 69. Stuttgart, Karlsakademie. Dining hall of Duke Eugen, built by R. F. Fischer. 1774-1775.

was the restoration of all things, the great homecoming. "Where are we going? Always home." Novalis was not the only one who had this deep feeling about life.

What these artists pictured is always only a piece of the earthly world, accessible to the senses, something completely earthly. If their landscapes light up with a spiritual, super-earthly quality, it is not because they turned away from the earth, but because they turned toward it and came nearer to it than ever before. For Ascension is not away from the earth but toward it. This lives in these pictures as a nearness which is sometimes almost alarming and oppressive, not unnatural, but supernatural.

It is what Brentano noted the moment he saw his first picture by *Caspar David Friedrich*, "Monk by the Sea." In a discussion of it he pointed out that it "has nothing in the way of a foreground but the frame." All of his pictures lack a foreground, more or less. They begin, as it were, on too high a level. Without any introduction they are suddenly just "there," quite near. This can be experienced most strongly in the case of Friedrich's self-portrait, which practically thrusts itself into the viewer. By this means, however, the viewer himself becomes the foreground, being pulled right along into the picture. The path leading into the snow-covered forest of pines, into the early morning mountain landscape, up to the city with the sun rising behind it, is the one I am standing on myself. This path does not invite us to walk on it; it is being walked on the moment we look at the picture.

This nearness can also be found in such pictures as *Philipp Otto Runge's* "Well," "The Hülsenbeck Children," "Morning," and others, where we can look into the large blossoms "from very near." This "nearness" is the most elemental expression of the fact that man is now awakening to an awareness of the place to which the Baroque was on its way, arriving, in other words, at the "interior space of the outer world," the point where inner space grows over into the outer world.

For inner space, inhabited inner space, is what is dawning in these pictures with such quiet grandeur. Their nearness is inner nearness. There is nothing in these pictures but the quiet presence of mountain, forest, sea and flower, but this stillness is pregnant with Word. This presence is an event and "almost becomes a face" (Rilke), an unfathomable countenance.

The verse by Novalis,

> "From herb, stone, sea and light's pure glance
> Shineth His childlike countenance,"

is something felt deeply from the very heart of Romantic landscape painting. A greater "I am" is dawning within the earth (Plate 70).

The place, however, where the earth breaks open toward the inside is man himself. (Goethe: "Is not the core of nature in the heart of man?" Novalis: "Man and world are two integral halves." Philipp Otto Runge: "For all the animals and the flowers are only half there as long as man does not add the best.") Man is the threshold over which the earth breaks open into the eternal and becomes "whole."

This is the significance of C. D. Friedrich's famous "figure seen from behind." The two friends gazing into the light of the rising moon, the girl at the window, the shepherd under the oak tree, the woman reading on the castle terrace, the wanderers on the chalk coast of Rügen, the girls among the darkening hay stacks: they are all thresholds over which we step into the inner space of these landscapes and over which the landscape itself whispers the secret of its existence back to us (Plate 71).

This "threshold" can be experienced especially strongly in the picture of the "Castle Terrace" with the reading woman. The low wall of "her" garden is not the only threshold; she herself is one as well, and across it the whole summer becomes a kind of house in which she lives. How narrow the house of Hieronymus was by comparison! How far the threshold has moved now! And yet the inner space has become no less significant and remains just as inhabited.

These figures are nothing but threshold. Unmoving as they face the landscape, they are turned toward it with the same full and absolute devotion as that with which the priest, the congregation and, indeed, the whole cathedral were turned toward the Gothic altar. Shining forth from it all is the priesthood of man, his priestly calling on behalf of the earth.

For the outward, visible earth *is* not heaven, nor *is* it of divine descent. Heaven has yet to rise within it; its divine essence is "enchanted" and needs to be "redeemed." If the painter does not see anything "in himself, he should stop painting what he sees in front of him. Otherwise his pictures will seem like screens, behind which one expects to find only the sick or even the dead" (C. D. Friedrich). For the world as outer world, the world of appearances, is sick and destined to die. "When the devil first burned up the earth and imprisoned the poor Soul so deep down within its darkness, God let the light go out, and now it (the Soul) is yearning for the light . . ." "Right in the center of the earth sits the poor Soul, longing for the light, just as we long to be in it. This is how the earth takes shape, like the embryo in the egg, and when the great

223

birth takes place, it will be redeemed" (Philipp Otto Runge). Here again the motif rings out of the homecoming of all things, of the unsealing and redemption or restoration of this hidden being to its true significance. It is a homecoming, but into something that still lies in the future, just as, to stay with the image of the fairy tale, the redeemed princess never returns to the house of her father but to "the other kingdom" of the son who has redeemed her.

At its roots, however, all this is the great mystery of the Last Supper, the transformation of the earth, the breaking open of what is earthly, to the end that the divine countenance slumbering within it may reveal itself.

The Apocalypse and the Völuspa contain the same secret of the new heaven and the new earth which are beginning to rise. "For the first heaven and the first earth have passed away."

The Romantics did not paint saints or scenes from heaven; they painted only the earth. Nevertheless, the subject of their representations was always God. They encountered the tremendous reality of God. They experience the cosmic fullness of the Sun-Word whose whisper penetrates their hearts and which rises now, not out in the cosmos, but within the earth, our earth. As Philipp Otto Runge was feeling his way toward the representation of Christ, he painted Him in a characteristic way: the first time, as the child who lies on the earth during the "Flight into Egypt," stretching out His little arms and looking up with His strange, deep, serious eyes at the light-beings who rise out of the open blossoms of the tree above Him and seem to be like Him in origin; the second time, as the One walking in majesty across the sea from the opposite shore on a trail of light.

Christ as the Coming One, Christ as the being whose "childlike countenance" is rising out of the earth, this alone is the God whom these people were able to experience with their deep, warm, honest hearts. Christ opens the rising inner space of the world.

The New Beginning

What lived in the Romantics was a premonition of things to come, but not much more than this. They were the last to participate in this unin-

Plate 70. Philipp Otto Runge (1777-1810). "Morning." Hamburg, Kunsthalle.

terrupted flow of vital, spirit-filled creativity, the last, but at the same time harbingers of the future as well. It seems at first that with them everything has come to an end. The heritage which mankind had received for so many thousands of years of its development and which had been the source of its life is all used up.

What comes after the Romantics, in the midst of a steadily increasing intellectualism and materialism, is the dreary emptiness of historicism, which had already begun in their time with the Nazarenes and continued on in the "Neo-Gothic" churches, in houses with Renaissance facades, etc.; other examples of it are the historical paintings that anxiously hide their inner smallness behind the outer dimensions of giant canvasses, the prettiness of genre painting, the dull spiritlessness of realism, the sentimentalities of "poetic" or "pious" scenes, the attempt of all these to hide their hollowness and futility under magnificently entwined decorations or the "brown sauce" skimmed off the great Dutch paintings of the 17th century. It is the deepest twilight of the gods which mankind had ever experienced. Had the Romantic vision been an illusion?

At the end of the seventies a movement begins which survives all the contempt, ridicule and hostility directed against it and soon swells to a powerful storm that sweeps away everything in its path. The age of the "isms" begins that supplant one another in dizzying succession (Impressionism, Neo-Impressionism, Pointillism, Symbolism, Expressionism, Fauvism, Futurism, Cubism, Surrealism and so on). We must not let all this confuse us. There is a danger in all these names that they will conceal the actual events behind a curtain of abstractions. If we look purely at the realities, the artists and their works, we can see that this was a unified movement expressing itself in a thousand variations. On the other hand, these things show that in an entirely different way than ever before the search was now on for consciousness in artistic creativity.

The new way of seeing and creating form which we associate with the concept of "modern art" makes its appearance in two great waves. The first one begins in the eighties of the previous century, and is identified with the names of *Cézanne, van Gogh, Gauguin, Hodler* and *Munch*. A second one follows it after the turn of the century, ushered in by *Matisse*,

Plate 71. Caspar David Friedrich (1774-1840). "Woman at the Window." 1822. Friedrich's wife is represented here in his studio on the bank of the Elbe. Berlin, Nationalgalerie.

Braque, Picasso and *Delaunay*. It includes many others who were either contemporaries of theirs or came later. The fact that we still experience this movement as "modern" art, even though its beginnings lie three full generations before our own, is a sign that it opened up a whole new cosmic space on mankind's path and was the decisive beginning of a completely new era.

The first step taken on the new path, or rather, the one which opens the new path and new living-space (*Lebensraum*), is the acknowledgement of what *is*. This means the admission that tradition is no longer a sustaining force and that no amount of looking backward to a great past will be of any help for the future. It is a confession of poverty. This experience had already surfaced with Caspar David Friedrich and Philipp Otto Runge; now it becomes a fact. It is now an absolute conviction that the world of "classical antiquity," the world of Greece and Rome—the highest standard and source of inspiration for all previous centuries—no longer opens up new pathways. But this is true of all tradition. Christianity, which still carried the Romantics as a matter of course, is also in question now. Man no longer finds anything in his environment to shelter and protect him. This cannot be taken seriously enough, for it means that in the full sense of the word the time is now beginning in which man must find the source of his inspiration and his standard within himself alone and can recognize no other.

The *Realists* as well as the *Impressionists* had actually already taken this step. The fact that man no longer has anything he can rely on except himself and his own senses was already the source of their creative power. But they had not yet experienced what that meant in the depths of their human nature. This is why the real breakthrough into the new did not take place with them.

Van Gogh then took the decisive step. In him, what the new situation of destiny was exacting from mankind became an experience that permeated the whole of his being. This is the reason for van Gogh's inner attraction to the new proletarian class arising just then. The proletarian is the person who has no heritage, who no longer has anything, in fact, except himself. If he felt "disinherited," this was true in a deeper and more tragic sense than he himself realized. If he regarded this as his own special destiny incurred by others, he was simply mistaken. For in reality what expressed itself in him, on all levels of existence, was only the same thing which a fearful and inwardly dishonest "middle class" of people refused

228

to acknowledge but which had long since actually become the destiny of *man*. The human being of this age is man *vis-à-vis du rien*—man face to face with nothingness. We must come to see what tremendous inner heroism and deep humility it signifies if the ideal to which the artist now turns as his highest goal is no longer called "beauty" but bears the name of "truth."

The result of this was that the painter began to choose subjects which in themselves were in no way "beautiful." Van Gogh showed a certain preference for poor, bent farmers, workers, women and children emaciated from their heavy toil. He would paint them as they worked or ate or rested; or he would paint the ugly modern industrial landscape, suburban streets and so on. For this is just what the world we must acknowledge as our own is like: poor, old and ugly.

But this is only one side of the reality. For now the miracle occurs. Beginning at a certain moment of his life, which has to be considered the moment of his actual, higher awakening, this very man, bowed down as he was to poverty and darkness, as well as all his work, are suddenly plunged into an immeasurable flood of glowing light.

We will never come anywhere near the mystery and the essence of our time until we see that it lives within the most tremendous tension that has ever been, the nature of which we can only attempt to convey by calling it "apocalyptic." Many people have had a living awareness of this. Such an awareness once led the great English writer, Charles Morgan, to have two of his characters say in a conversation:

"But listen . . . this is the twentieth century! Have you noticed what has happened in Germany and Russia?"—"Yes," she said, "and also in Babylon and Tyre."

What does this mean? Nothing less than the fact that what is being experienced is, on the one hand, the decline of a world and the emergence of the most tremendous destructive forces, while on the other, as depicted in the Book of Revelations, it is basically all just the prelude to, and the sign of, the radiant rise of a whole new world. When *Rudolf Steiner*, the most wide-awake spirit of our century, said that today it is mankind's destiny to "cross the threshold" as a whole, this is the same thing, seen from the human side. For it means that now mankind as a whole is undergoing what single individuals experienced in former times behind the protective walls of mystery temples: death and resurrection. Experiences of death and destruction begin to spread with an intensity never before imagined. But so do the experiences that death is but the prelude to resurrection, as poverty is the prelude to unimagined wealth.

The miracle that now occurs is that out of the very darkness and poverty van Gogh felt moved to acknowledge so deeply, there suddenly dawns this infinitely radiant light. Van Gogh once wrote to his brother, ". . . I should like to paint men and women with this eternality whose sign used to be the halo and which we now seek in the radiance and glow of our colors." And this is how he painted them. On another occasion he wrote, "If I stay here (in the south), I will not try to paint a Christ in the Garden of Olives, but rather the olive harvest the way it looks now; and if I can find the true proportions of the human figure in it, it will be possible to think of the former scene while looking at this one." If we only take seriously what he is trying to say, it can only mean that what was formerly experienced as the Beyond, for which one could only set a sign, begins to break through into the Here and Now and that the Eternal—heaven and its most lofty spiritual being—is beginning to rise in the midst of the poverty and ugliness of our present age. What is transfigured in the most radiant way is ugliness itself, which he embraces with a genuine love. "I have never," so he wrote, "had such good help as what came to me through this ugly, worn out woman. To me she is beautiful . . . She has been ploughed, and this is why I find more in her than in a whole series of unploughed ones." Ploughed, like the dark earth. He is the human being who declares his total allegiance to the earth and to its depths. It is no accident that the same motifs of the ploughman, the sower and the reaper recur again and again in his pictures. From now on, what Goethe had stated in his novel, *Wilhelm Meister's Years of Travel*, is true for the artist as a principle of his creative work:

"But now it is necessary to speak about the third religion, based on the reverence for what is underneath us; we call it the Christian one, because such a way of thinking is most evident in it; it is a final stage to which mankind had to come, and did. But how much is involved in not only leaving the earth behind and looking up to a higher place of birth, but also in acknowledging meanness and poverty, scorn and contempt,

Plate 72. Vincent van Gogh (1853-1890). "The Sower." 1888. Zürich, donated by Bührle.

disgrace and misery, suffering and death as things divine, and in revering and loving even sin itself and crime, not as hindrances, but as things that further what is holy!"

This is what van Gogh experienced. Transfiguration is no longer an article of faith or a sentimental feeling; it becomes experience. For the light that shines out of his pictures with such overwhelming power has risen out of the deep darkness into which his early works are plunged without exception. What shines there with such purity is always the Easter light rising from the grave. Transfiguration is already poured out over the little tree in blossom in the poor suburban court, as well as over the sower, this crude peasant who strides across the broken soil in front of the huge rising sun and is painted in such a way that we are made to wonder whether God is not a peasant after all (Plate 72). His "Raising of Lazarus" shows that he must have at least surmised the mystery of this light, for he painted the sun in this picture at the very spot where Christ should actually be standing. The Resurrection light, the light of the Transfiguration, whose power to call forth from the grave had become for him an experience that permeated all earthly being, is the Christ. Not the Christ of the church. For him the Christ of tradition is dead.

It is clear now that the Romantics had seen correctly when they represented Christ as the Coming One. It is just that now, as this coming takes place, it is infinitely more powerful than what they had sensed and prophesied.

Ego-Mysteries

What, then is the organ with which the new world is experienced? Where is the "threshold" which man must cross to meet it? Asking this question, we encounter the same mystery, but one layer deeper. The place of transfiguration and of inspiration is the very one which was first experienced as the place of death: the human ego. From now on, no work of art will come about if the artist merely looks at his object from the out-

Plate 73. Paul Cézanne (1839-1906). "Landscape near Aix." New York, Metropolitan Museum.

232

side. The truly creative act is experienced in a process which may be thought of as "saying 'I' to" or "identifying oneself with" the object. Paul Cézanne was the other great and lonely figure of those years who, just as alone and aroused by virtually the same morning call, also struggled to find the new word (which was still the same word, although it took on a different sound with him). He once said that "the landscape mirrors itself, thinks itself within me . . . Perhaps this is all nonsense, but it seems to me as though *I myself were the subjective consciousness* of this landscape . . ." (Plate 73).

What is meant by this is not what man usually refers to as the "I," or ego, which is the very thing that must be silent. "But if he (the artist with his everyday consciousness, that is), intrudes, if he, poor wretch, dares to interfere consciously in the process of translation, he will only bring his own personal unimportance and insignificance into it; the work becomes inferior . . . His entire willing must be silent. He must silence all voices of prejudice within himself, forget, forget, make silence, be a perfect echo."

He knows that this human ego must be prepared for this, which is why elsewhere he says, "I told you before that the unprejudiced brain of the artist must be like a photographic plate, sensitive to light . . . But through baths, wisely and according to plan, this plate was brought to a degree of sensitivity at which it can saturate itself conscientiously with the image of things. Long work, meditation, study, joy and sorrow, life itself have all prepared it." The ego as the center of the whole human being is the instrument of artistic creativity that has to be "prepared." If this is done, a greater ego can rise within it that says "I" to the earth.

Here again we find ourselves in the midst of an apocalyptic experience. For, behind this "I, and yet not I," can we not hear that other word, "Now I live, yet not I, but the Christ in me"? Perhaps we must say that we hear it from very far away. But what is beginning to be fulfilled in our time will never be understood so long as we do not open our ears to these spheres as well.

The transition from the "wretched," "insignificant" ego to the other one which has the power to become a threshold becomes visible in a dramatic way in the case of van Gogh. It is especially striking how frequently the motif of the bridge occurs in his pictures during the early part of his years in Arles, the first time his genius was able to really assert itself. Certainly problems of painting were what motivated him here. But besides this it is surely no accident that this particular motif was the one that aroused his interest. It is important to view this against the background of a night some five years earlier in which he had lost his way in a storm while wandering across the Dutch heath. Later on, at home, he wrote to his brother Theo that "(life is) a terrible reality, and we are traveling to infinity; what is, is, and the way we understand it does not take anything from it or add anything to the essence of things . . . It is damned miserable, brother!" That was what he was suffering from to the point of despair and madness in those years of dark and uncertain inner turmoil. What he was experiencing within himself was the destiny of mankind, the fact that man has become an ego-being, detached from the world; but as a result he has also become a prisoner, locked up within himself, unable to get across to the things themselves—"it is damned miserable, brother!" And now the bridge that leads across! For the fact that it was built is attested to by everything he paints from this point on. The foundation, however, on which it is built is that heightening and stimulation of his ego, about which he writes on one occasion that it can intensify to the point of unconsciousness, or again, to such "terrible clairvoyance," in which he is nevertheless fully awake and sober at the same time and has to "think of a thousand things in half an hour," in "sober work and calculation."

Once more a word becomes audible behind all this: "I am the door."

And a further mystery is touched on. This ego is no mere spectator. What Cézanne meant by the "perfect echo" or the photographic "plate" must not be understood in a passive sense. The inner attitude and the inner process involved in this are of the highest activity. "Whoever wishes to create in an artistic way must follow Bacon," he said, "who defined man as *homo additus naturae* . . . Our task is to make her (nature's) eternity visible." Van Gogh said the same thing in almost the same words: "Art is man added to nature, which he delivers."

Delivers—that means that what is going on is a birth-process. A "new" earth, the first one to be really "real," wants to come into being, and the artist is its midwife. In his creating a higher creating reveals itself, a creative process in which what is brought to birth is more than just a new picture. It is an act of knowing, but a "knowing" in the sense of the Old Testament, where "to know" is the same as "to procreate." "And Adam knew Eve his wife; and she conceived, and bare . . ." This is why Cézanne spoke again and again of the endless effort it takes to *réaliser*. It

235

was his experience that something "real," an objective, spiritual-physical entity, wants to come into being. This is the sense in which another sentence of van Gogh's is to be understood: "All the paintings I made from nature were chestnuts that I snatched from the fire." The agonizing intensity of this process could not be described any better. A fire-process is at work, in which the "eternality" of imperishable nature is being "delivered." Cézanne, who was granted a life of almost seventy years, in contrast to van Gogh, who was burnt out after not much more than three years of real productivity, was at least sometimes aware that with all this much more was at stake than the human aspect. As he once remarked to Gasquet, "The nature we see and the nature we feel, the one out there and the one in here (he strikes his forehead), both must permeate each other in order to last, to live; a half human, half divine life; the life of art, get this, the life of God!"

This must be taken as seriously as it was said and meant. Cézanne knew what he was saying. "The life of God" was not just a nice phrase for him but a perceptible reality, *the* reality. Did he not once, when he was to paint Clémenceau, break off the sittings with the question, "Is it possible to paint a human being who does not believe in God?" He saw that "the life of God" was not in this man, and he was neither willing nor able to paint a world in which it was not present. In such cases there was nothing there for what was active in him as creative energy to enter into a conversation with.

We can see from this that not only transfiguration but resurrection, too, becomes perceptible as objectively real corporeality made of spirit. A "new heaven" and a "new earth" begin to rise in our midst. That, too, becomes experience. "Behold, I make all things new!" as the writer of the Apocalypse hears Him who is the resurrection say.

The life of God was what all these pioneers of a new world were seeking, Gauguin (Plate 74) as well as the others, whether they knew it or not. It was breaking through to them on all sides through cracking walls. Something that they all had more or less in common is a completely new relationship to light. The light that illuminates objects from without no longer plays a role in their pictures. The colors glow out of themselves with a light they bear within them. What Philipp Otto Runge and Goethe

Plate 74. Paul Gaugin (1848-1903). "Contes Barbares." 1902. Essen, Volkwang-Museum.

had discovered in a more theoretical way, that color is a kind of being or "a power of nature in itself," is something they not only recognize anew but also practice. The strong pure colors of their pictures are rediscovered words of creation. A world of light is "delivered." The "light of the world" rises from within.

As with the colors, so with the forms. With Gauguin, Hodler and Munch lines suddenly acquire a life of their own which is full of strong expression, greater and more mysterious than anything "straight from nature." Are they not the gestures in which the creative "life of God" reveals itself, the arrested traces of His movement? We find this same line of thinking in Cézanne's statement that everything in nature is built on the sphere, the cone and the cylinder. What he experienced was a great and sacred order within the forms of creation. "God mathematizes."

It was the experience of the pure colors and these large, simple forms that later made it possible for Gauguin to paint the South Sea Islanders, a people still woven into the life of cosmic powers in a deeply dreaming way and in whose flower-like lives the ancient gods still dream.

In all these individuals a process is beginning which goes far beyond the single human being and his intentions. Something like a higher will becomes perceptible at work within it all. Wherever we may turn now in our time, words become audible which until now resounded from much farther away. For our world, what in former times had only lived in the sphere of faith begins to become experience. May we not, then, recognize, in that fire-process that van Gogh spoke of, the fire of which He said that He had come "to cast it upon the earth," as well as the fire of the spirit which flamed up over His disciples at Whitsuntide?

Today He can become visible everywhere, He who acknowledged the earth so deeply, who "identified" himself completely with the earth at the Last Supper and on Golgotha set His seal on this act of "saying 'I'" to the whole earth; He, under whose hands a new life and a new reality began to come about.

Rilke's Ninth Duino Elegy is a magnificent expression of what all of the above has attempted to describe:

"Praise the world to the Angel . . .
Tell him the things . . .
. . . These things that live on death

understand, that you praise them; fleeting
they rely for rescue on us, the most fleeting of all.
Want us to change them entirely in our invisible hearts,
in—oh, unending—in us! Whosoever we may be in the end.

Earth, is it not this that you want: invisibly
arising in us? is it not your dream
to be one day invisible?—Earth! invisible!
What is your urgent command, if not transformation?
Earth, you loved one, I will . . .
Nameless I am committed to you, from far away.
. . . . ."

(Adapted from the translation of J. B. Leishman and
Stephen Spender)

In the great letter to his Polish translator, Rilke expressed how terribly seriously he wished this to be taken, so seriously, in fact, that he came to the following tremendous insight: "Thus, in this way we prepare not only intensities of a spiritual nature but, who knows, new bodies, metals, galaxies and celestial bodies." In the same letter he also writes, "But not in the Christian sense (which I am growing away from with increasing fervor), but rather in a purely earthly, deeply earthly, sublimely earthly consciousness is it necessary to introduce what has been seen and touched on *here* into broader, indeed the broadest possible surroundings. Not into a Beyond whose shadow darkens the earth, but rather into a whole, into the whole." If Rilke can write such a thing as this, it means that he is a witness to the Christ, only not in the sense of a traditional Christianity which seeks the One it venerates in the same place where the Middle Ages experienced Him. For He has long since gone on further, and it is true for many people today, as it was in the times of early Christianity, that they meet and serve a God whose name they do not know, "the Unknown God." It can be recognized that today, as then, this is none other than the One who through the ages travelled toward the earth and now begins to rise within it as a new heaven and a new earth.

Egypt had experienced Him as the world-creator in whose word, whose breath and pulse-beat all His creatures live, including man as His creation. But a new age is now beginning in which man must experience himself as something more than a mere creation. Within his own inner being the creative power begins to rise. He himself becomes a creator.

And, like the primal fire out of which the world came into being, the fire from which the new world is proceeding burns. It burns within the hearts of men. It burns within the "I" in which the Christ is living.

World Inner Space

What had started with van Gogh, Cézanne and Gauguin continues on with the second wave in which modern art advances. Only now it is as though a curtain has again been torn apart and humanity has passed through a second, inner portal, all the way into the new land.

With Cézanne, van Gogh and Gauguin something had begun which is now brought to its ultimate conclusion. With the passage of time, the (apparent) dimension of depth of the picture had become less and less important. Matisse as well as the German Expressionists had continued this development. But then, with Braque, Picasso, Delaunay and *Juan Gris*, something happens that cannot be described as anything else but the shattering of space. It splinters into surfaces that shove themselves into each other but are no longer stretched out into the third dimension (Plate 75). They are like "windows," a name Delaunay gave to a whole sequence of pictures. But through these windows we do not look into earthly space. Where do we look?

From the beginning of the Renaissance on, painters had more or less always had the ideal of painting things and people the way they *look*, or appear, or perhaps also the way they appeared to them. But now *Franz Marc*, whose genius had been enkindled in the encounter with this new world that had first been transmitted to him by *August Macke*, wrote to his wife, "I never, for instance, have the urge to paint animals 'the way I see them,' but rather the way they *are*." He explains this by saying, "The way they themselves look at the world and feel their being." And he found the image that could express what he meant by this in a more living way than any other. It came to him one day as he caught sight of a

Plate 75. Georges Braque (1882-1963). "Violin and Jug." 1910. Basel, Öffentliche Kunstsammlung.

waterfowl diving into the water at a certain place, and, later on, ". . . its enraptured surfacing somewhere else; realize, my friends, what pictures are: something emerging or coming to the surface somewhere else." And this is how, showing them emerging within these pictures, he painted the magnificent horses with their rhythm of cosmic vitality; the beloved deer with their shy, graceful frailty; the bull like a mountain range of quiet, self-contained strength; the danger-filled, steel-like hardness of the tiger crouching tensely in ambush. He painted them as they are in their world, a very different one from ours. He painted them in their deep inter-wovenness with the nature that not only surrounds them but of which they are a part. From an even greater inner depth he was able to paint the infinite melancholy of the living creature and its "anxious hope" for release and awakening from bondage to eternal, unchanging law. This was the origin of the "Tower of the Blue Horses" (Plate 76).

There is no better way of expressing what lives in these images and thoughts and is striving to make itself known here than with the words from another poem by Rilke:

"Throughout all beings extends one space, world inner space . . ."

World inner space is the space into which Delaunay's "windows" also look. Van Gogh's bridges led to it as well, and the Romantics had already felt its breath. What takes form in all these pictures and experiences is not, as it might first seem, a denial of what man had achieved at the beginning of the modern age. It is the continuation and fulfillment of it all. World inner space is the space which grew and grew in the buildings of the Baroque. Rembrandt and the other Dutch artists were knocking at its door. Now it has been reached and entered.

Another expression of the fact that this has happened is that *perspective* has also lost its former validity, which had been attained at the time when man was beginning to perceive himself as the center of the world and to see the world "from his own standpoint." This standpoint is outside the world, facing it. Now, however, the ego has also entered this world inner space into which the world is rising. The concepts of "far" and "near" take on a different meaning.

Now there can also be such a thing as a "time-perspective," for not only has space shattered without a sound; time, too, has melted away.

Plate 76. Franz Marc (1880-1916). "The Tower of the Blue Horses." Burned in 1910 in the fire of the Glass Palace in Munich.

This not only means that a picture may contain a mixture of views that could normally only be had one after another—profile and full face, for instance—but also that both past and future are alive in the present.

One way in which this can appear is in the form Picasso gave it, where in one picture the weight-bearing foot of a runner is still enormous while the head is quite small, as though it were already far off in the distance. Another way is with *Chagall* (Plate 77), in whose work freedom from time (*Zeit-Entrückung*) is an especially prominent feature.

"World inner space"—in the prologue of the Gospel of St. John there is a sentence pregnant with this mystery. Luther's translation reads, "who is in the Father's lap." Literally translated it would be: "the one (who is) being 'into' the bosom (lap or womb) of the Father," which means that He is the place where the Father stands open toward the inside. World inner space: where the world has been broken open like the host in the mystery of the transsubstantiation.

Paul Klee must also have known something of the Logos-mystery of this sphere. Somewhere he asks, "Who would not like to live as an artist at that point where the central organ of all movement in space and time, whether we call it the brain or the heart of creation, calls all functions into being? In the womb of nature, in the primal ground of all creation where the secret key to everything is kept?"

It is characteristic of Klee that he is more sensitive to the mystery of the creation of the outer world by means of the Logos. What speaks more strongly through August Macke, on the other hand, is the mystery of the New World which is coming into being within world inner space. What lives in his gleaming pictures, in which man and world appear as though new born in the colorful clouds of light of a new day of creation, Macke himself once expressed by saying, "I wanted to permeate the world with joy." The world, not only the people in it! And permeate it with joy, not just make it happy! This "new" world is not a dead one, filled with indifferent laws; it is ensouled, permeated with breath. And when we stand before his pictures, we also know that the joy of which he spoke and which truly breathes through them is not just common, everyday happiness. It is that holy joy, beyond all suffering and death, of which the Conqueror of death had spoken. At the moment when He himself was about to enter suffering and death, He called this "going to the Father." At that time His deed laid the foundation for what Goethe calls in the passage quoted earlier ". . . recognizing suffering and death as something divine . . ." This holy joy is His breath and the pulse of His life. It is the world's deepest Inner Space.

Apocalyptic Decision

Mankind is crossing the threshold. This alone is the aspect from which modern art is to be understood, especially what has appeared of it since the turn of the century.

There is a frequently quoted remark by Paul Klee to the effect that it is not the task of art to "reproduce what is visible," but to "make visible." This was always the case, of course. Art always made something visible which "would have remained invisible without it," as Goethe put it. But for the modern age this is true in an entirely different sense.

In former times, all art was a message from the gods, revealing itself in the radiance of beauty, in harmony and in correct proportions. To be sure, the world of physical appearances was the curtain through which they would whisper their message to whoever would listen, but the creative powers themselves, who had woven the curtain, remained hidden behind it. Paul Klee is speaking about this crossing of the threshold when he says, ". . . he (the artist) is more concerned about the formative forces than he is about the finished forms . . . The more deeply he looks at a finished image from nature, the stronger is his impression at that point of the essential image of creation as a process of genesis; this is the only image that matters." What Klee means is that a world which is actually invisible by its very nature, the creative world of the spirit, wants to become visible so that it can be experienced.

The overcoming of what is at first visible by this other, "invisible" world—the shift of balance, in other words, in favor of what wants to become "visible"—had already begun with Cézanne. It then became the predominant factor in the late work of van Gogh, in whose trees, clouds and revolving stars and suns these very "formative forces," "creation as a process of genesis," were already pushing their way into visibility. But this development continued on as the forms of the visible world disappeared more and more, to the degree that lines and colors came to be experienced as original forces or even as revelations, gestures of the crea-

tive powers. In this experience we find the roots of non-objective art. "Arsenal of a Creation" is the title of a picture by Franz Marc in which, in "spaceless space," there appear nothing but pointed, round or angular forms, circles, spirals, etc.; actually, such forms are not even present, but only their beginnings. What Goethe once characterized as the essence of Bach's music by saying that it was "how things might have been in God's bosom right before the creation of the world" is raised to the level of visibility in Franz Marc's painting.

Erhart Kästner's beautiful words about the pictures of Paul Klee also speak of this crossing of the threshold: "These pictures were obviously the attempt to paint things whose home is in the world between sleep and wakefulness." This means that they signify an awakening into the world which is otherwise concealed under the mantle of sleep, the world which we "enter every night" (Morgenstern). Paul Klee himself said, "On this side of life I cannot be understood at all, for I am just as at home among the dead as I am among the unborn. Somewhat closer to the heart of creation than usual. But not yet close enough by far."

But what he expressed this way, which was chosen as his epitaph, is true today for all of us. It is just that we fail to notice it. As Franz Werfel once wrote, "We live in the midst of the kingdom of God and are not aware of it" (Plate 78).

But not only in the kingdom of God.

The most formidable confirmation of the fact of the crossing of the threshold, if not the most convincing one, is that now the dark abysses of the drama of the Apocalypse are beginning to open up on every side and that they, more than anything else, do so in a heretofore unprecedented fashion.

One often gets the impression that what is emerging now are the dark counter-images of light-filled forms which had truly pointed to the future. What had opened the kingdom of the heavens to van Gogh had been his acknowledgement of poverty. He was the beggar, but a beggar for the spirit. Whenever he painted what was ugly, he seemed to be saying at the same time, "This is not the final word!" In contrast to this, there were those who made it their task to unmask the apparent orderliness of the world and to unveil the ugly, the animal-like and the demonic which lurk everywhere at its foundations. Pictures like this made *George*

Plate 77. Marc Chagall (b. 1899). "Peasant Eating." Drawing from about 1913.

Grosz and *Otto Dix* famous. They are indictments of a corrupt, decaying society. But is this really the task? In the "Prologue in Heaven" of his *Faust*, Goethe showed that he knew as well as the author of the Apocalypse that the one who "day and night accuses man before God's throne" is not the angel, let alone the Christ. It is Mephistopheles, the dragon. Offense, not compassion, is the source of all these pictures.

If the ego is considered the actual location of the threshold, the counter-image of this can be found in many manifestations of Expressionism. *Meidner, Kokoschka* and even many of the pictures of *E. L. Kirchner* can be mentioned in this connection. In its inmost being, the "elemental" which they desire to praise is of the same nature as the abyss itself. But neither the crampedness nor the ecstasy with which they seek to force the boundaries open is the way to the heightened ego.

A matter of much more serious concern, because it is harder to see through, is everything that has appeared, and continues to appear, as the counter-image of the other side of this mystery, the ". . . but not I." The first thing to consider in this connection is everything that goes by the name of *"Surrealism"*: the pictures of *Max Ernst, Chirico, Dali* and many others. Here certain people have become channels of a spirituality that denies anything that has to do with the ego at all. Max Ernst once speaks of the "fairy tale of the artist's creativity" as the "ultimate superstition" and demands a "purely passive role of the 'author' in the mechanism of poetic inspiration." Apollinaire coined the phrase of the "psychic automatism" for this. At any rate, what emerges in their pictures now is something which has never existed before. Many artists have painted hell, but what these artists paint is worse: the landscape of never-ending desolation, of the last and final death in which there is nothing left but ghosts.

Here, too, it is a question of something far greater than man, only now in the sense of a lower, sub-natural world. If pictures like these have moved people to speak of a "pathos of absurdity," this dreadful expression is true at least to the extent that a throne has been prepared here for the "spirit who forever denies." *

Here, too, there are endless variations. But basically it is the same ice-

*Mephistopheles, in Goethe's *Faust*.—tr.

Plate 78. Hermann Kirchner (1899-1978). "Golgatha." 1945. India ink drawing.

249

cold face that looks out at us from paintings inspired by the world of machines (*Léger*) and from much of the "abstract painting" (by *Mondrian* and others). For the various tensions, differentiations of emphasis, etc., which are naturally present in them breathe an icy indifference as well.

This is where the totally and decisively different situation in which the modern artist finds himself comes into view, the artist, that is, in the age in which mankind begins to cross the threshold. For never before has it been the case that it was possible to be an artist and at the same time to open the gates to the powers that destroy. Until now he, too, was protected like the rest of humanity, in the sense that great and friendly spirit beings would work through him, if only he were truly an artist. The entrance to the garden in which God dwells was closed to mankind. But an angel was there who kept it closed with the same sword he also used to seal off the gates of hell. And the artist who came near this threshold had no other words to proclaim than the ones this being had whispered to him. Now, however, he has stepped aside. The door stands open. The gods, but also the demons, are beginning to become visible and active among us.

To prove or deny the reality of the spiritual world has long since ceased to be a problem of timely concern. In every single one of its manifestations, modern art proves that the world of the senses is only foreground and that the spiritual world is the real, essential one.

The real and most important problem of today is this, that it is both expected of, and entrusted to, man to take over the office of the guardian himself, which the great angel occupied for so long a time. It is now up to man himself to discriminate and to decide. It is no longer enough for a man to experience the supersensible world in such a way that it merely stirs his soul; to have a contact with it, in other words, which is merely an artistic inspiration. He is expected to distinguish what region the spirit who has touched him belongs to. More than ever before, what is artistic is not only an *esthetic* question, but a *moral* one as well. Not "moral" in the sense of middle-class morality, but in the sense of such questions as these: What sort of will is at work in you? Who within you is saying "I" to you?

Cézanne who knew so much, touched on this mystery once in one of his strangest sentences. He was speaking to Gasquet about the sun and about how all things and all living beings, including ourselves, are nothing but stored-up sun, "a remembrance of the sun." And he went on to say, "Perhaps the moral force distributed over all the world is only man's striving to become sun again."

He must have sensed something of the great mystery, of the great Sun-Being by whom all things were made and who united himself in unending love with man and with the earth, of man's calling to transform the earth, and even of the sunrise out of the earth.

For this is what is at stake today.

APPENDIX

NOTES

INDEX

APPENDIX

Comments on Chapter III

". . . the strength of many thousands . . ."

In the rock tomb of Thuthotep, the county prince of Bersche (12th dynasty), there is a picture of the transportation of a 6.5 m high statue of the prince, which is described in the accompanying text as follows:

"The path along which the statue arrived was difficult beyond description . . . My heart rejoiced. All the inhabitants of the town shouted with joy. It was beautiful beyond description . . . Even children and old people lent a hand to demonstrate their reverence to their beloved sovereign. Eagerness doubled the strength of all . . . their arms grew strong, and each one had the strength of many thousands . . ."

This text provides an answer to the question of how the Egyptians managed to move the statues, the obelisks, etc., which were often such enormously heavy loads. We today are still aware that people who lose their normal, everyday consciousness (the mentally ill, epileptics, etc.) suddenly develop tremendous strength. The riddle is solved if we assume that the Egyptians lived in a state of consciousness which was not nearly as strongly connected with the earth as our consciousness is today, so that they were not at all "within themselves" in the same way as yet and could get "out of themselves" much more easily, as this text describes it. We may add that they had quite specific means (rhythmic songs, incense, etc.) of achieving such a "loosening."

Pyramid Texts
Which Describe the Path of the Deceased

"How beautiful it is to behold, how wonderful to see, when you ascend to the everlasting stars. Thus you go to your mother, the goddess of heaven, Nut. She summons for you the gods who dwell in the sky, and they unite themselves for you with the gods who dwell on the earth, so that you may be with them and may stride upon their arms. King Unas has come to his throne, and he appears in the likeness of a star."

———

"He found the gods standing, wrapped in their garments, wearing white sandals upon their feet. They threw their sandals aside; they took off their garments. 'Our heart was not glad until you came,' they said . . ."

———

"The portal of heaven is open for you, and the great bolts are pulled away from you. There you find Re standing; he takes you by the hand, leads you to the sacred place of heaven and seats you upon the throne of Osiris, upon this your brazen throne, that you might reign over the blessed ones . . . The servants of the god stand behind you, and the nobles of the god stand before you and call, Come, you god! Come, you god! Come, you owner of Osiris's throne! Isis speaks to you and Nephthys greets you. The blessed ones come to you and bow down to kiss the earth at your feet. Thus you are protected and adorned like a god, clothed in the figure of Osiris, upon the throne of the first of those who are in the west. You do what he did amongst the blessed and the immortal. You let your house blossom behind you, and you guard your children against anxiety . . ."

The Problem of Chronology

It is not possible to date the reigns of the kings of the first dynasties with absolute accuracy. The statements of scholars on this point vary by several centuries. If a certain system of dating is adhered to here which puts the kings of the fourth dynasty, i.e., the great pyramid builders, some 200 years earlier than is generally done today, this is not done without good reason or in ignorance of the problem. If dates are doubtful, "inner" viewpoints should at least be permitted to have their say.

The sudden appearance of the urge to build pyramids, as well as its equally sudden disappearance and the emergence of the sun temples, established boundaries which cannot be overlooked and whose roots can be seen clearly in spiritual realms. There is not the slightest reason to believe that external events had any part in this. They are boundaries in a sense similar to that of the two other "cosmic" transitions, which are more obvious to us: the one from the Egyptian to the Greco-Latin cultural epoch and the one from the Greco-Latin to our own. In these instances it is clearly evident that the cutoff years, which correspond to the cosmic dates, are 747 B.C. and 1413 A.D. and not 200 years later.

For this reason it would be a good idea to examine whether the older calculation with the dates mentioned in our text is not the more correct one.

It is true for both the beginning of the age of the pyramids with Djoser and his great "Master Builder" Imhotep (behind whom one of the greatest initiates of Egypt seems to be hidden) and for the transition from the second to the third Sothis period, in the 5th dynasty, that certain changes occur in the deepest layers of humanity and that the transformations of artistic impulses are only "manifestations" of these changes. It is also evident here that the impulse does not come from outside. Thus E. Otto writes in his excellent book, *Ägypten, Der Weg des Pharaonenreiches* (*Egypt, the Path of the Kingdom of the Pharaohs*, Stuttgart, 1953, untranslated), ". . . It is certain that no outer influences can be cited as causes of this; neither can one speak of an exhaustion of the state and of its means . . . nor of a hostile attack from any enemy which might have resulted in a collapse . . . The crisis is indeed a total one, since it has an equal effect on the economy and the religion, the government and the community, and on the totality as well as on each individual . . . Thus the viewpoint of the Egyptian seems justified after all, that in the final analysis a cosmic catastrophy of mythical dimension is involved, a kind of Twilight of the Gods . . ." (p. 93).

The same author (p. 91) describes the inner side of this transformation as "a step from out of the magical, super-individual relationships of life in the direction of a step-by-step evolution of self-consciousness on the part of man."

This "Twilight of the Gods" is a part of the mystery of the Bird Bennu, of the death and rebirth which stands out so clearly in the rhythm of the Sothis periods. It is quite natural that processes should be involved here which run their course over centuries. Nevertheless, everything is grouped around one or the other of these points of juncture.

The drama of the transition from one Sothis period to another is even greater the next time it occurs. Beginning with Amenophis I (1557-1530)

257

and advancing from sovereign to sovereign, one could point to the definite progression toward a new threshold which each time appears to derive from a super-personal, goal-directed consciousness. Personal experiences of a calling: in the case of Thutmose III through an image of a god in the temple, in the case of Thutmose IV in a dream; the enhancement of personal self-awareness on the basis of personal abilities; the new custom of visiting ancient tombs and temples because of their special beauty (and therefore no longer because of their cultic significance); descriptions of scenes from the private life of the pharaoh on commemorative scarabs (under Amenophis III; with Amenophis IV they are already becoming large wall-reliefs)—all this and much more speaks clearly enough of the new Twilight of the Gods, of a grasping of the earth and a withdrawal from the world of the gods in a manner unthinkable in earlier times. The growth of outer power, leading to the establishment of Egypt as a world power, is also evidence of this. If one then considers the time of the Ramessides, i.e., the first two centuries of the fourth Sothis period, as the age of "personal piety," what has happened becomes absolutely clear. But when, at about the same time, not only piety but hypocrisy as well can be noticed and the first satire and obscene drawings begin to appear, it becomes apparent how Egypt loses its spiritual content around this time. The gold and silver temple vessels which contained the life of the gods are no longer in the country. The mythical history of the Old Testament depicts events of Egypt's spiritual history here whose truth is patently evident. (Elsewhere I have described in detail the extent to which forerunners of the transition from the bronze age to the iron age play a part in these events. See *Die Christengemeinschaft* 28, 12.)

Comments on Chapter V

The Pectorius Inscription

The Musée Rolin in Autun (France) owns an inscribed tablet of priceless value from the 2nd century which was found in a cemetery in the 19th century. Probably it was originally a stone slab on a grave and contains, in the Greek language, lines in verse form which sound as if they were the words spoken at the communion of believers. After these comes the actual epitaph. Few things exist through which blows so noticeably the breath of an age in which the portals toward "the other side" stood so wide open. As was the custom at that time, the name of Christ appears under the emblematic word, "Ichthys" (fish).

"Receive, o mortal, as a divine child of the heavenly fish and with a heart inspired by awe, the gift of immortality. Rejuvenate your soul, friend, in the divine water, in the inexhaustible fountain of wisdom. Receive the honey-sweet nourishment, which the Saviour of the hallowed ones presents. Eat and drink; you hold the Ichthys in your hands.

Ichthys, lord and master, bestow upon me the grace which I most anxiously desire, that my mother may rest in peace. For this I beseech you, you light of the dead. And you, Aschandios, my father, whom together with my sweet mother and my brothers I tenderly love, remember your son Pectorius in the peace of Ichthys."

NOTES

1 Cf. in particular, besides the works of Rudolf Steiner: E. Bock: *Urgeschichte (Genesis)*, Edinburgh: Floris Books, 1983; R. Karuts: *Das Rätsel des Janus (The Riddle of Janus)*, untranslated; G. Wachsmuth: *Werdegang der Menschheit (The Evolution of Mankind*, Dornach, Switzerland: Philosophisch-Anthroposophischer Verlag, out of print).

2 We call the organism of these upbuilding forces of life in the body the "etheric body."

3 One must not equate what is indicated here with the modern theory of biological descent. For one thing, the Egyptian did not arrive at such knowledge on the basis of external observation, but from inner experiences in a deep, dreamlike condition; for another, he did not understand what he learned in this way in any materialistic sense, but as a process which was predominantly spiritual.

4 The term "soul body" refers to the organism of the soul's forces, the bearer of conscious awareness, feelings, urges, desires and fears. In spiritual science it is also called the astral body, since forces from the world of the stars express themselves in it.

5 4th ed., Stuttgart, 1975.

6 Only by understanding this can we also understand the role that the never-ending service of the dead played in Egypt, which nearly turned the whole country into an enormous cemetery. A very large part of the country did, in fact, belong to the dead. It was their property and their legacy. From it came the ceaseless sacrifices which maintained both the priesthood and the religious centers. If, in the reliefs and paintings that decorate the walls of the burial chambers, we find not only those figures represented who bring sacrifices to the gods and the dead, but also the farmer, the hunter, the fisherman, the craftsman, etc., we should not view this as a sentimental reminder of the life that the deceased has left behind. It means that everyone involved in the continuous effort to serve the dead is shown.

A story has been preserved from about 2000 B.C. that casts light on all this. Sinuhe, a teller of tales, has been forced to flee the country because of certain questions of dynastic succession that never quite come into focus. At the high point of his extremely successful life abroad he is overcome by an irresistible longing to return home again, not to live there, but to die. One can live anywhere. But one can only die in the right way in Egypt.

For the Egyptian, the "right" way to die, which properly integrates the human being into the cosmic world order, was connected with the affirmation of the physical body. This is the secret of the mummy cult.

7 Lipit Ishtar, about 2100 B.C.: Meri-Ka-Re, 2070-2041.

8 The dates of 2782 for the transition from one Sothis period to the next and 2750 for the change of dynasties do not coincide in an exact mathematical sense. On the one hand, however, the dating of anything Egyptian before 2000 is uncertain and can vary by as much as 100 years. On the other, dates such as those of the Sothis periods are only ideal dates anyway which processes in real life can only approximate. No child gets his second teeth exactly on his 7th birthday, nor does he attain physical maturity the day he turns 14. Nevertheless, it is a fact that human life develops according to a 7-year rhythm. With regard to Egypt, we are forced to acknowledge that the coincidence is surprisingly exact after all.

9 The terrace temple which Mentuhotep III had already built near Deir-el-Bahri around 2050 and which is often regarded as a predecessor or even a model for the structure Queen Hatshepsut erected demonstrates precisely by its apparent relationship and external similarity how new what Hatshepsut intended actually was. The culmination of the Mentuhotep structure is the pyramid that stands inside the second courtyard as the tomb of the king—a structure built entirely in traditional form. The temple of Hatshepsut actually has the queen's funerary chapel within those parts of it that have been driven deep into the rock. But her grave is not there; it is in the mountain range behind it, as a rock tomb in the Valley of the Kings.

10 Alfred Stange: *Das frühchristliche Kirchengebäude als Bild des Himmels* (*The Early Christian Church Building as an Image of Heaven*), Cologne, 1950, untranslated.

11 "I believe, that I may understand" and "I understand, that I may believe."

12 This has been described in greater detail in the author's book, *Chartres—Die Herrlichkeit der Kathedrale* (*Chartres, the Magnificence of the Cathedral*), 4th ed., Stuttgart, 1976, untranslated.

13 The archetypal character of the Palestinian landscape is one of the great discoveries of E. Bock. Cf. especially his *Kindheit und Jugend Jesu* (*Childhood and Adolescence of Jesus*), 4th ed., Stuttgart, 1956, untranslated.

INDEX

(Page numbers of illustrations are in boldface)

Bach, Johann Sebastian 247
Bacon, Francis 235
Baldung Grien, Hans **193**, 197, **199**, 200
Bamberg 135
Baptism, see Christ, John the Baptist
Barfield, Owen xi
Baroque 109, 203ff., **206, 209**, 219, 242
Basilica xiv, 3, 114ff., **115, 117**, 122f., 130, 158f., 163f., see Early Christian art
Beauvais (cathedral choir) 150
Beethoven, Ludwig van 157
Bennu 44ff., 61, 64, 71, 256, see also Bird
Bethlehem 191
Bible 30, 35, 108, see also Gospel of St. John, Moses
Bindel, Ernst 36, 53
Bird(s) **27**, 28, 41, 43ff., 58, 61, 64, **66**, 71, 256, see also Bennu
Birth of Aphrodite (Ludovisian Throne) 82, **83**
Birth of Christ (Baldung Grien) **192**
Block statue 69, **70**
Bock, Emil 107, 259, 260
Böhme, Jacob 204, 217
Bosch, Hieronymus 194, **195**
Braque, Georges 228, 240, **241**
Breasted, J.H. 59
Brentano, C.v. 222
Bruckner, Anton 157
Bruyn, Bartholomäus 200
Buddhist temple, see India (temple)
Bull (Taurus) 41ff., 52, 104ff., **105**, 184f., 242, see also Apis bull
Burial stele 47, **102**, 103

C

Caesar 58, 69, 110, 113, 119, 171
Castle Terrace (Friedrich) 223
Catacombs 114

Cathedral xiv, 2, 122ff., 154, 157, 159f., 162, 172f., 187, see also Gothic cathedral, Romanesque cathedral
Cella 80, **81**, 119
Celtic 123, 139ff.
Centaur 89ff., 92f., 102, 105
Central type of building 114f., **117, 118**, 121, 123, 171, **172**
Cézanne, Paul 227, 232, **233**, 235ff., 240, 245, 250
Chagall, Marc 244, **246**
Chahar-Bagh **153**
Charioteer 89, 98f., 102, 105ff.
Charioteer (Delphi) **90**
Chartres 135, **143**
Chefren, see Khephren
Cheops 50, 58, 64; pyramid 37, 50, **51, 54**
Chephren, see Khephren
China, Chinese 4ff.; temple 4ff., **5, 6**
Chirico, Giorgio de 250
Chiron 93, see also Centaur
Choir, choir gallery 124, 126f., 130, 146, 150
Chrétien de Troyes 143
Christ xivf., 15, 107f., 141, 150, 194, 215, 225, 230ff., 239f., 250, 259; ascension 107, 215f., 222; baptism 107; birth **192**; death xiv, 107, 150, 156; incarnation xivf., 154; passion 194, 200; resurrection xiv, 107, 156, 200, **201**, 215, 232, 236; see also Last Supper, Mystery of Golgotha, Sun god, Word
Christian, Christianity xii, xv, 114, 120, 152ff., 156, 159, 163, 167, 186, 228, 239, see also Early Christian art
Christian Community xii
Christmas 191, 194, 200
Chronos 83
Church, see Cathedral, Hall church, House of God, Temple
Circus 111

F

Feet   10, 183f.
Ficino, Marsilio   83
Fischer, R.F.   **221**
Flight into Egypt (Runge)   225
Flying Buttresses, see Piers
Forum   111
Fouquet, Jean   187
France   143ff., 163, 169, 187, 257
Freiburg im Breisgau   135, **147, 148**
French Revolution   219
Friedrich, Caspar David   222, 223, **226**, 228
Futurism   227

G

Gablik, Suzi   xi
Galilee   191
Gallery   **118**, 125, 158, see also Triforium Gallery
Gasquet, Paul   236, 250
Gate   6, 7, 38ff., see also Door, Portal
Gate of Ishtar   **40**
Gauguin, Paul   227, 236, **237**, 238, 240
Geb   31, 33f., **34**
Geb-el-Adde   65
Germany, Germanic   xii, xiv, 3, 110, 123, 129, 141, 143ff., 163f., 169, 174ff., 219, 229, 240
Gilgamesh   39
Giza   **23, 28, 42, 50, 54**
Goethe, Johann Wolfgang von   ix, xii, xiv, 3, 28, 72, 84, 207, 213, 223, 230, 236, 245ff.
Gogh, Vincent van   227ff., **231**, 238, 240, 242, 245, 247
Gold background   116, 179, 181, 214f.
Golgotha (Kirchner)   **248**
Gospel of St. John   31, 106, 244, see also Word
Gospel of St. Luke   63

Gospels   107, 108
Gothic   xiv, 122, 135, 137, 143ff., 152ff., 158f., 163ff., 169, 173, 211, 223, see also Late Gothic
Gothic cathedral   3, 122, **136, 138, 142, 147, 148**, 150, 158, 163ff.
Gottfried of Strasbourg   135
Grail, see Holy Grail
Grave   36, 41, 43f., 47, 58, 68f., 71, 75, 79, 111, 113, 155f., 194, 200, 219, 231, see also Burial stele, Tomb
Greece, Greek (Hellenistic)   xv, 32, 45, 59, 72ff., 84ff., 89ff., 99ff., 104ff., 107, 109ff., 123, 129ff., 141, 144, 169, 171, 174f., 183ff., 189ff., 219, 228, 257
Greek temple   xivf., 3, 75ff., **77, 81, 101**, 119, 124, 129, 132, 149, 158, see also Apollo, Hephaestus, Zeus
Gris, Juan   240
Grosz, George   249
Group sculpture   174
Grünewald, Matthias   194, **196**, 200, 201, 203

H

Hall church   164, **165**, 167f., 173
Halle en der Saale   166
Hammurabi   39
Haremhab   65
Hathor   19f., 21, see also Horus
Hatshepsut   65, 261
Heavenly Jerusalem   159
Hegel, G.W.F.   xv
Heliopolis   30f.
Hellenistic Baroque   109
Hephaestus, temple   **77**
Hera   79
Heretics   67, 149, 152
Hestia   **82**
Hieroglyph   27, 30, 62, 186
Hieronymus in the Cell (Dürer)   180, **182**, 223
High altar   171

Photograph Credits: Fratelli Alinari, Florence: 3, 29, 52, 53; Bavaria Verlag, Munich: 8, 14, 46; Werner Blaser, Basel: 1; F. Bruckmann, Munich: 54, 55, 56, 57, 58, 59, 60, 61, 62, 66, 67, 68, 70, 71, 72; Deutsche Fotothek, Dresden: 10, 64, 73, 74; Hirmer Fotoarchiv, Munich: 5, 7, 9, 13, 18, 19, 20, 21, 22, 23, 24, 25, 27, 28, 30, 31, 32; Martin Hürlimann, Zürich: 2; Landesbildstelle Württemberg, Stuttgart: 44, 47, 49, 51, 63, 69; Foto Marburg, Marburg: 6, 10, 16, 33, 34, 35, 36, 37, 38, 39, 43, 65, 76; Staatliche Antikensammlung und Glypthothek, Munich: 17; Willy Pragher, Freiburg i.Br.: 42; Bildarchiv Preußischer Kulturbesitz, Berlin: 46; Martin Sandkühler, Stuttgart: 45; Frank Teichmann, Stuttgart: 4; from the author: 75, 77, 78